The Science of
GETTING
RICH
in
MARRIAGE

SACHA MUHAMMAD

Book design and layout by Sacha and Sherman Muhammad (www.enjoymentcounselor.com).

Published by
JOUISSANCE PUBLISHING

Copyright © 2010 Sacha & Sherman Muhammad
All rights reserved.

ISBN: 1452844097
ISBN-13: 9781452844091
Library of Congress Control Number: 2010906333

To Our Children

Amira

Aqueil

Cheyenne

Maryam

Safiyyah

Naeema and Bilal

You are our greatest accomplishment.

There is nothing you cannot have or be if you
take the time to think, act, and do.

May your thoughts come true.....

We would like to express our deepest gratitude
to God for His mercy and beneficence.

Table of Contents

Forward

After learning the Certain Way to Tranquility, the Certain Way to Tranquility stands correct. You can demonstrate it at no limit of time. Then you must learn to use it in a way to bring you the desires of your heart. Let us see ourselves in heaven at once.

The intent of this book is to help couples see success in marriage and life. For couples to find the road to improve their union with each other. After realizing, we had traveled so many years in our marriage being on two different roads, but our desires were the same. We wanted exactly the same things. However, we were competing for whose road or whose way we would take instead of making our thoughts one and moving forward. We thought how many other marriages were going through the exact same thing and wondering isn't there more to this marriage thing?

What we found was that when we took the time to act deliberately and put our efforts together on a creative plain instead of competing with one another on any level caused the desired effect in getting us what we were trying to achieve. We got what we wanted! We reasoned that you must think and act in a Certain Way in your marriage.

You have the power of two. The power of two creative souls to bring what you think about into reality. The power of two minds to help bring into fruition that which is impressed upon Formless Substance the "Everything". Along with working on ourselves individually, there is a need for positive imagery to see ourselves in our marriages happy, healthy, and wealthy and with the expressed desire to have more. By being married, we announce to the Universe that we are making room in our lives for the one we say we love.

"For this reason a man will leave his father and mother, and be united to his wife, and they will become one flesh." Gen 2:24

There are different circumstances that come with being married. To get rich and have the desires of your heart when you are in a relationship takes double the work. You both have to make the effort to share and keep the complete vision in your thoughts. There are different needs that have to be addressed in a relationship where the consideration for both has to be present. To harness and learn to use the Will of two souls is a real and strenuous work. Noble and respected is the couple who will take the time to look into their relationship to see if there are any ills to cure.

"Never let us be discouraged with ourselves. It is not when we are conscious of our faults that we are the most wicked; on the contrary, we are less so. We see by a brighter light; And let us remember for our consolation, that we never perceive our sins till, we begin to cure them".
– Fenelon

How do you help one another with what is called the "Push" in your relationship? To actively listen to one another and incorporate two thoughts into one thought that will benefit and make both of you happy and rich.

To bring your blueprint into reality, you must have the faith to see beyond what current appearances suggest. No matter what comes know that there is a successful path to take, so that your marriage stays on track to a fulfilled union. To show sincere gratitude for all that is and will be. In addition, to be grateful before your thoughts become tangible is a work like no other. Put it in a marriage and you have the makings of a real workout. However, when you find yourselves doing what is prescribed in this book you will undeniably get rich in life and marriage.

There is opportunity to improve ourselves alone as individuals and we should, however, there is another thought that holds weight in our world. Therefore, make sure to always include each other in thought, we believe that these principals should be written and directed toward people, in relationships and couples in marriage seeking a more abundant existence.

What we know is that when you think on a thing, you have the ability to bring the things you think about into concrete reality. With the power of two how much more, can you bring to your marriage? You must concretize your thoughts and you have to see a complete vision with details. The wording in this print is to reflect that with the power of two souls any marriage can bring what they think about into existence.

We made the deliberate effort to create the image of you as a couple in how you can apply these principals to your marriage. As you read, we want you to have the ease of seeing yourselves as a couple in a successful and healthy marriage. The best way to help the world is to get better in every area of you lives.

Love flourishes best in refinement

See yourself better,
Sherman and Sacha Muhammad
Authors

Here is the syllabus:

There is a Thinking Stuff from which all things are made, and which, in its original state, permeates, penetrates, and fills the interspaces of the Universe. A thought in this substance produces the thing that is imaged by the thought.

Husband and wife can form things in their thought, and by impressing their thought upon Formless Substance can cause the thing they think about to be created.

In order to do this, husband and wife must pass from the competitive to the creative mind; otherwise, they cannot be in harmony with the Formless Intelligence, which is always creative and never competitive in spirit.

Husband and wife may come into full harmony with the Formless Substance by entertaining a lively and sincere gratitude for the blessings it bestows upon them. Gratitude unifies the mind of man and woman with the intelligence of Substance, so that their thoughts are received by the Formless. Husband and wife can remain upon the creative plane only by uniting themselves with the Formless Intelligence through a deep and continuous feeling of gratitude.

Husband and wife must form a clear and definite mental image of the things they wish to have, to do, or to become; and they must hold this mental image in their thoughts, while being deeply grateful to the Supreme that all their desires are being granted to them. The couple who wishes to get rich must spend their leisure hours in contemplating their Vision, and in earnest thanksgiving that the reality is being given to them. Too much stress cannot be laid on the importance of frequent contemplation of the mental image, coupled with unwavering faith and devout gratitude. This is the process by which the impression is given to the Formless, and the creative forces set in motion.

The creative energy works through the established channels of natural growth, and of the industrial and social order. All that is included in their mental image will surely be brought to the man and woman who follow the instructions given above, and whose faith does not waver. What they want will come to them through the ways of established trade and commerce.

In order to receive your own when it shall come to you, then man and woman must be active; and this activity can only consist in more than filling their present place. They must keep in mind the purpose to get rich through the realization of their mental image. And they must do, every day all that can be done that day, taking care to do each act in a successful manner. They must give to every man, woman and child a use value in excess of the cash value they receive, so that each transaction makes for more life; and they must so hold the Advancing Thought that the impression of increase will be communicated to all with whom they come in contact.

The men and women who practice the foregoing instructions will certainly get rich; and the riches they receive will be in exact proportion to the definiteness of their vision, the fixity of their purpose, the steadiness of their faith, and the depth of their gratitude.

PREFACE

This book is pragmatic, not philosophic; a practical manual, not a treatise upon theories. It is intended for the men and women whose most pressing need is for money; who wish to get rich first, and philosophize afterward. It is for those who have so far found neither the time, the means, nor the opportunity to go deeply into the study of metaphysics, but who want results and who are willing to take the conclusions of science as a basis for action, without going into all the processes by which those conclusions were reached.

It is expected that the reader will take the fundamental statements upon faith, just as he and she would take statements concerning a law of electrical action if a Marconi or an Edison promulgated them; and, taking the statements upon faith, that he will prove their truth by acting upon them without fear or hesitation. Every man or woman who does this will certainly get rich; for the science herein applied is an exact science, and failure is impossible. For the benefit, however, of those who wish to investigate philosophical theories and so secure a logical basis for faith, I will here cite certain authorities.

The monistic theory of the Universe the theory that One is All, and that All is One; That one Substance manifests itself as the seeming many elements of the material world is of Hindu origin, and has been gradually winning its way into the thought of the western world for two hundred years. It is the foundation of all the Oriental philosophies, and of those of Descartes, Spinoza, Leibnitz, Schopenhauer, Hegel, and Emerson.

The reader who would dig to the philosophical foundations of this is advised to read Hegel and Emerson for himself.

In writing this book, I have sacrificed all other considerations to plainness and simplicity of style, so that all might understand. The plan of action laid down herein was deduced from the conclusions of philosophy, it has been thoroughly tested, and bears the supreme test of practical experiment; it works. If you wish to know how the conclusions were arrived at, read the writings of the authors mentioned above; and if you wish to reap the fruits of their philosophies in actual practice, read this book and do exactly as it tells you to do. - Wallace D. Wattles

The Right to be Rich In Marriage

Whatever may be said in praise of poverty, the fact remains that it is not possible to live a really complete or successful life in marriage unless you are rich. No marriage can rise to its greatest possible height in talent or soul development unless they have plenty of money; for to unfold the soul and to develop talents within marriage, a couple must have many things to use, for they cannot have these things unless they have money to buy them with.

A marriage develops in mind, soul, and body by making use of things, and society is so organized that you must have money in order to become the possessor of things; therefore, the basis of all advancement for marriage must be the science of getting rich.

The object of all life is development; and everything that lives, has an inalienable right to all the development it is capable of attaining.

A couples right to life means their right to have the free and unrestricted use of all the things, which may be necessary to their fullest mental, spiritual, and physical unfoldment; or, in other words, the science of getting rich in marriage.

In this book, we shall speak of riches in a figurative way and in a literal way; to be really rich does not mean to be satisfied or contented with a little. No marriage ought to be satisfied with a little if they are capable of using and enjoying more. The purpose of Nature is the advancement and unfoldment of life; and every marriage should have all that can contribute to the power, elegance, beauty, and richness of life; to be content with less is *sinful*.

The marriage that owns all they want for the living of all the life they are capable of living is rich; and no marriage that has not plenty of money can have all they want. Life has advanced so far, and become so complex, that even the most ordinary man or

1

woman requires a great amount of wealth in order to live in a manner that even approaches completeness. Every person naturally wants to become all that they are capable of becoming; this desire to realize innate possibilities is inherent in human nature; we cannot help wanting to be all that we can be. Success in life is becoming what you want to be; you can become what you want to be only by making use of things, and you can have the free use of things only as you become rich enough to buy them. To understand the science of getting rich in marriage is therefore an essential piece of knowledge.

There is nothing wrong in wanting to get rich. The desire for riches is really the desire for a richer, fuller, and more abundant life; and that desire is praise worthy. The couple who does not desire to live a more abundant life is abnormal, and so the couple who does not desire to have money enough to buy all they want is abnormal.

There are three motives for which we live; we live for the body, we live for the mind and we live for the soul. No one of these is better or holier than the other one; all are alike desirable, and no one of the three, body, mind, or soul can live fully if either of the others is cut short of full life and expression. It is not right or noble to live only for the soul and deny mind or body; and it is wrong to live for the intellect and deny body or soul.

We are all acquainted with the loathsome consequences of living for the body and denying both mind and soul; and we see that real life means the complete expression of all that man and woman can give forth through body, mind, and soul. No couple can be really happy or satisfied unless their bodies are living fully in every function, and unless the same is true of their minds and souls. Wherever there is unexpressed possibility, or function not performed, there is unsatisfied desire. Desire is possibility seeking expression, or function seeking performance. A couple cannot live fully in body without good food, comfortable clothing, and warm shelter; and without freedom from excessive toil. Rest and recreation are also necessary to their physical life.

They cannot live fully in mind without books and time to study them, without opportunity for travel and observation, or without intellectual friendships at home and abroad.

To live fully in mind they must have intellectual recreations, and must surround themselves with all the objects of art and beauty they are capable of using and appreciating.

To live fully in soul, a marriage must have love; and love is denied, expression by poverty.

A couple's highest happiness is found in the bestowal of gifts and benefits on those they love and each other; love finds its most natural and spontaneous expression in giving. The man and woman that have nothing to give cannot fill their place as a husband and wife or mother and father or as citizens. It is in the use of material things that a couple finds full life for their bodies, develops their minds, and unfolds their souls. It is therefore of supreme importance that a couple should be rich.

It is perfectly right that you should desire to be rich in your marriage; if you have a normal marriage, you cannot help doing so. It is perfectly right that you should give your best attention to the science of getting rich in marriage, for it is noble and necessary of all studies. If you neglect this study, you are derelict in your duty to yourself, to God and humanity; for you can render to God and humanity no greater service than to make the most of yourself and your marriage.

NOTES

RICHES ARE NOT AND END TO LIFE,
BUT AN INSTRUMENT OF LIFE
– H.W. Beecher

There is a Science to
Getting Rich in Marriage

There is a science to getting rich in your marriage, and it is an exact science, like algebra or arithmetic. There are certain laws, which govern the process of acquiring riches and having the marriage you desire. Once these laws are learned and obeyed by any couple, they will get rich and improve their union with mathematical certainty.

The ownership of money and property comes as a result of doing things in a *Certain Way*; those who do things in this Certain Way, whether on purpose or accidentally, get rich; while those who do not do things in this *Certain Way*, no matter how hard they work or how able they are, remain poor.

It is natural law that like causes always produces like effects therefore any man and woman who learn to do things in this Certain Way will infallibly get rich and have a happy and healthy marriage.

That the above statement is true and shown by the following facts:

Getting rich is not a matter of environment, for, if it were, all the people in certain neighborhoods would become wealthy; the people of one city would all be rich, while those of other towns would all be poor; or the inhabitants of one state would roll in wealth, while those of an adjoining state would be in poverty.

However everywhere we see rich and poor living side by side, in the same environment, and often engaged in the same vocations. When two people are in the same locality, and in the same business, and one gets rich while the other remains poor, it shows that getting rich is not, primarily, a matter of environment. Some environments may be more favorable than others may.

When two marriages are in the same business of being married and one thrives while the other fails, it indicates that getting rich and having the relationship you want is the result of doing things in a *Certain Way.*

And further, the ability to do things in this *Certain Way* is not due solely to the possession of talents, for many marriages that have great talent remain poor, while others who have very little talent get rich.

Studying the marriages that are wealthy, successful, and healthy, we find that they are an average lot in all respects, having no greater talents and abilities than any other marriage. It is evident that the success of the relationship is not because they possess talents and abilities that other marriages do not, but because they happen to do things in a *Certain Way.*

Getting rich is not the result of saving, or "thrift"; many very penurious marriages are poor, while free spending marriages often get rich.

Nor is improving your marriage due to doing things which others fail to do; for two couples married for the same length of time often do almost exactly the same things, and one is rich, healthy and passionate while the other remains poor, weak and becomes emotionally bankrupt.

To be truly rich means you cannot be content with a little.

From all this we must come to the conclusion that getting rich is the result of doing things in a Certain Way. Being rich in marriage, results in two people doing things in a *Certain Way.*

If getting rich in your relationship is the result of doing things in a *Certain Way,* and if like causes always produce like effects, then any couple that can do things in that way can become rich in their marriage, and the whole matter is brought within the domain of exact science.

The question arises here, whether this **Certain Way** may not be so difficult that only a few may follow it. This cannot be true, as we have seen, as far as natural ability is concerned. Talented couples get rich, and blockhead couples get rich; intellectually brilliant couples get rich, and very stupid couples get rich; physically strong couples get rich and weak and sickly couples get rich.

Some degree of ability to think and understand is, of course, essential; however in so far as natural ability is concerned, any man and woman in marriage that has sense enough to read and understand these words can certainly get rich and enjoy a fulfilled and happy marriage.

We have seen that it is not a matter of environment. Location counts for something; one would not go to the heart of the Sahara Desert and expect to do successful business. Getting rich involves the necessity of dealing with people and of being where there are people to deal with; and if these people are inclined to deal in the way you want to deal, so much the better. However, that is about as far as environment goes.

In your marriage there has to be a partnership. You would not expect to have an affectionate and interactive marriage living on two different continents. Nor can you desire to be intimate three times a week when you are gone from home six nights or work until exhaustion. Let alone be spontaneous.

If anybody else in your town can get rich and live in a healthy marriage, so can you; and if anybody else in your state can have a rich and fulfilled marriage, so can you. Couples are not rich and healthy because of any physical features or monetary holdings. A marriage is rich and successful because they do things in a **Certain Way**.

It is not a matter of choosing some particular business or profession. People get rich in every business, and in every profession; while their next-door neighbors in the same vocation remain in poverty. There are successful marriages in every class, creed, color, and race.

It is true that you will do best in a business, which you like, and which is congenial for each of you and if you have certain talents, which are well developed, you will do best in your relationship when you can exercise your talents.

Just like you will do best in a business, which is suited to your locality; an ice-cream parlor would do better in a warm climate than in Greenland, and a Coffee Shop will succeed better in a neighborhood, than atop Mount Everest, where there are no people.

However, aside from some general limitations, getting rich in marriage is dependent upon learning to do things in a **Certain Way**. If you are now in a marriage, and there are marriages of the same duration that are successful, while your marriage is not, it is because you are not doing things in the same way that the other couples are doing them.

No one is prevented from getting rich by lack of capital. True, as you get capital the increase becomes more easy and rapid; however, one who has capital is already rich, and does not need to consider how to become so. No matter how poor you may be, if you begin to do things in the **Certain Way** you will begin to get rich; and you will begin to have capital. The getting of capital is a part of the process of getting rich; and it is a part of the result, which invariably follows the doing of things in the **Certain Way**. You may be the poorest couple on the continent, and be deeply in debt; you may have neither friends, influence, nor resources; but if you begin to do things in this **Certain Way**, you must infallibly begin to get rich, for like causes must produce like effects.

If you have no capital, you can get capital; if you are in the wrong business, you can get into the right business; if you are in the wrong location, you can go to the right location; if you don't have the marriage you want you can create the marriage you want; and you can do so by beginning in your present state by do things in the **Certain Way** which causes success.

NOTES

A HAPPY MARRIAGE IS A NEW BEGINNIG OF LIFE, A NEW STARTING POINT FOR HAPPINESS AND USEFULNESS.
– A.P.Stanley

Is Opportunity Monopolized from Married Couples?

No couple is kept poor because opportunity has been taken away from them or because other people have monopolized love, peace, money, luxury, tranquility, good homes and joy nor have they put a fence around it to keep you from it.

Scenario:

The same way you may think you are shut off from engaging in business in certain lines, but there are other channels open to you. Probably it would be hard for you to get control of any of the great Banking systems; that field is pretty well monopolized. Nevertheless, the internet business is still in its infancy, and offers plenty of scope for enterprise. It will be but a very few years until collecting energy from the sun and high speed transportation through the Rail Road will become a great industry, and in all its branches will give employment to hundreds of thousands, and perhaps to millions, of people. Why not turn your attention to the development of an internet business, instead of competing with the software giants and others for a chance in the computer software world.

It is quite true that if you are a worker in the employ of the steel factory you have very little chance of becoming the owner of the plant in which you work. However, it is also true that if you will commence to act in a Certain Way, you can soon leave the employ of the steel factory; you can form an internet business, and engage in business as a producer or provider of information. There is great opportunity at this time for couples who will provide products and information on the internet; such couples will certainly get rich. You may say that it is impossible for you to start an internet business, but we are going to prove to you that it is not impossible and that you can certainly get an internet business or two or three internet businesses if you will go to work in a Certain Way.

11

At different periods, the tide of opportunity sets in different directions, according to the needs of the whole, and the particular stage of social evolution, which has been reached. At present, in America, it is setting toward information, renewable energy, and the technical industries and professions. Today, opportunity is open before the factory worker in his line. It is open before the businessperson who supplies the farmer more than before the one who supplies the factory worker; and before the professional person who waits upon the farmer more than before the one who serves the working class.

There is an abundance of opportunity for the couples who will go with the tide, instead of trying to swim against it.

Scenario:

So the fast food workers, either as individuals or as a class, are not deprived of opportunity. The workers are not being "kept down" by their masters; they are not being "ground" by the fast food industry and combinations of capital. As a class, they are where they are because they do not do things in a Certain Way. If the workers of America chose to do so, they could follow the example of their brothers in Belgium and other countries, and establish great department stores and co-operative industries. They could elect men of their own class to office, and pass laws favoring the development of such co-operative industries; and in a few years, they could take peaceable possession of the industrial field.

The working class couple may become the master class whenever they will begin to do things in a Certain Way; the law of wealth is the same for them as it is for all others. This they must learn; and they will remain where they are as long as they continue to do as they do. The working class marriage however, is not held down by the ignorance or the mental slothfulness of their class; they can follow the tide of opportunity to riches, and this book will tell them how.

No marriage is kept in poverty by shortness in the supply of riches; there is more than enough for all. A palace as large as the capitol at Washington might be built for every family on earth from the building material in the United States alone. And under intensive cultivation, this country would produce wool, cotton, linen, and silk enough to cloth each person in the world finer than King Solomon was arrayed in all his glory; together with food enough to feed them all luxuriously.

The visible supply is practically inexhaustible; and the invisible supply really is inexhaustible.

Everything you see on earth is made from one original substance, out of which all things proceed.

New Forms are constantly being made, and older ones are dissolving; but all are shapes assumed by One Thing.

There is no limit to the supply of Formless Stuff, or Original Substance. The Universe is made out of it; however, it was not all used in making the Universe. The spaces in, through, and between the forms of the visible Universe are permeated and filled with the Original Substance; with the Formless Stuff; with the raw material of all things. Ten thousand times as much as has been made might still be made, and even then, we should not have exhausted the supply of universal raw material.

No man or woman, therefore, is poor because nature is poor, or because there is not enough to go around.

Nature is an inexhaustible storehouse of riches; the supply will never run short. Original Substance is alive with creative energy, and is constantly producing more forms. When the supply of building material is exhausted, more will be produced; when the soil is exhausted so that food produce and materials for clothing will no longer grow upon it, it will be renewed, or more soil will be made. When all the gold and silver has been dug from the earth, if man is still in such a stage of social development that he needs gold and silver, more will be produced from the Formless. The Formless Stuff responds to the needs of couples; it will not let them be without any good thing.

This is true of man and woman collectively; the human race as a whole is always abundantly rich, and if individuals and marriages are poor, it is because they do not follow the Certain Way of doing things, which makes the individual man and woman rich.

The Formless Stuff is intelligent; it is stuff which thinks. It is alive, and is always impelled toward more life.

It is the natural and inherent impulse of life to seek to live more; it is the nature of intelligence to enlarge itself, and of consciousness to seek to extend its boundaries and find fuller expression. The Universe of forms has been made by Formless Living Substance, throwing itself into form in order to express itself more fully.

The Universe is a great Living Presence, always moving inherently toward more life and fuller functioning.

Nature is formed for the advancement of life; its impelling motive is the increase of life. For this cause, everything, which can possibly minister to life, is bountifully provided; there can be no lack unless God is to contradict Himself and nullify His own works.

Your marriage is not kept poor by lack in the supply of riches; it is a fact which we shall demonstrate a little farther on that even the resources of the Formless Supply are at the command of the man and woman who will act and think in a Certain Way.

NOTES

THE SECRET OF SUCCESS IN LIFE, IS FOR A PERSON TO BE READY FOR THEIR OPPORTUNITY WHEN IT COMES.

– Benjamin Disraeli

The First Principle in the Science of Getting Rich in Marriage

Thought is the only power that can produce tangible riches from the Formless Substance. The stuff from which all things are made is a substance which thinks, and a thought of form in this substance produces the form.

Original Substance moves according to its thoughts; every form and process you see in nature is the visible expression of a thought in Original Substance. As the Formless Stuff thinks of a form, it takes that form; as it thinks of a motion, it makes that motion. That is the way all things were created. We live in a thought world, which is part of a thought Universe. The thought of a moving Universe extended throughout Formless Substance, and the Thinking Stuff moving according to that thought, took the form of systems of planets, and maintains that form. Thinking Substance takes the form of its thought, and moves according to the thought. Holding the idea of a circling system of suns and worlds, it takes the form of these bodies, and moves them as it thinks. Thinking the form of a slow-growing oak tree, it moves accordingly, and produces the tree, though centuries may be required to do the work. In creating, the Formless seems to move according to the lines of motion it has established; the thought of an oak tree does not cause the instant formation of a full-grown tree, but it does start in motion the forces which will produce the tree, along established lines of growth. There is a path that thought has to travel with no shortcuts.

Every thought of form, held in Thinking Substance, causes the creation of the form, always, or at least generally, along lines of growth and action already established.

The thought of a house of a certain construction, if it were impressed upon Formless Substance, might not cause the instant formation, of the house; but it would cause the turning of creative energies already working in trade and commerce into such channels as to result in the speedy building of the house. And if there were no existing channels through which the creative energy could work, then the house would be formed directly from primal substance, without waiting for the slow processes of the organic and inorganic world.

No thought of form can be impressed upon Original Substance without causing the creation of the form.

Man and woman are thinking centers, and can originate thought. All the forms that man and woman fashion with their hands must first exist in their thoughts; they cannot shape a thing until they have thought that thing. And so far man and woman have confined their efforts wholly to the work of their hands; they have applied manual labor to the world of forms, seeking to change or modify those already existing. They have never thought of trying to cause the creation of new forms by impressing their thoughts upon Formless Substance.

When husband and wife have a thought-form, they take material from the forms of nature, and make an image of the form, which is in their mind. They have, so far, made little or no effort to co-operate with Formless Intelligence; to work "with the Father." They have not dreamed that they can "do what they seeth the Father doing." Husband and wife reshape and modify existing forms by manual labor; they have given no attention to the question whether they may not produce things from Formless Substance by communicating their thoughts to it. We propose to prove that you may do so; to prove that any marriage may do so, and to show you how. As our first step, we must lay down three fundamental propositions.

First, we assert that there is one original Formless Stuff, or Substance, from which all things are made. All the seemingly many elements are but different presentations of one element; all the many forms found in organic and inorganic nature are but different shapes, made from the same stuff. And this stuff is thinking stuff; a thought held in it produces the form of the thought. Thought, in thinking substance, produces shapes. Man and woman are thinking centers, capable of original thought; if man and woman can communicate their thought to original Thinking Substance, they can cause the creation, or formation, of the thing they think about. To summarize this:

There is a Thinking Stuff from which all things are made, and which, in its original state, permeates, penetrates, and fills the interspaces of the Universe.

A thought, in this substance, produces the thing that is imaged by the thought.

Husband and wife can form things in their thought and by impressing their thought upon Formless Substance, can cause the thing they think about to be created.

It may be asked if we can prove these statements; and without going into details, we answer that we can do so, both by logic and experience.

Reasoning back from the phenomena of form and thought, we come to one original Thinking Substance; and reasoning forward from this Thinking Substance, we come to a couple's power to cause the formation of the things they think about. And by experiment, we find the reasoning true; and this is our strongest proof.

If one couple who reads this book gets rich in their marriage by doing what it tells them to do, that is evidence in support of our claim; but if every couple who does what it tells them to do gets rich in marriage, that is positive proof until someone goes through the process and fails. The theory is true until the process fails; and this process will not fail, for every couple that does exactly what this book tells them to do will get rich in their marriage.

We have said that couples get rich by doing things in a Certain Way; and in order to do so, they must be able to think in a Certain Way.

A couple's way of doing things in their marriage is the direct result of the way they think about things in their marriage.

To do things in a way you want to do them, you will have to acquire the ability to think the way you want to think; this is the first step toward getting rich.

To think as a couple what you want to think is to think TRUTH, regardless of APPEARANCES.

Every man and woman has the natural and inherent power to think what he or she wants to think, but it requires far more effort to do so than it does to think the thoughts that are suggested by appearances. To think according to appearance is easy; to think truth REGARDLESS of appearances is LABORIOUS, and requires the expenditure of more power than any other work a couple, is called upon to perform.

There is no labor from which most people shrink as they do from that of sustained and consecutive thought; it is the hardest work in the world. This is especially true when TRUTH is contrary to APPEARANCES. Every appearance in the visible world tends to produce a corresponding form in the mind, which observes it; and this can only be prevented by holding the thought of the TRUTH.

To look upon the appearance of disease will produce the form of disease in your own mind, and ultimately in your body, unless you hold the thought of the truth, which is that there is no disease; it is only an appearance and the reality is health.

To look upon the appearances of poverty will produce corresponding forms in your own mind, unless you hold to the truth that there is no poverty; there is only abundance.

To look upon the appearances of divorce will produce corresponding forms in your mind, unless you hold to the truth that there is no divorce; there is only a loved filled marriage.

To think health when surrounded by the appearances of disease, or to think riches when in the midst of appearances of poverty, requires power; however, the couples who acquire this power become MASTER MINDS. They can conquer fate; they can have what they want.

This power can only be acquired by getting hold of the basic fact which is behind all appearances; and that fact is that there is one Thinking Substance, from which and by which all things are made.

Then we must grasp the truth that every thought held in this substance becomes a form, and that man and woman can so impress their thoughts upon it as to cause them to take form and become visible things.

When we realize this, we lose all doubt and fear, for we know that we can create what we want to create; we can get what we want to have, and can become what we want to be. As a first step toward getting rich in marriage, you must believe the three fundamental statements given previously in this chapter; and in order to emphasize them. We repeat them here:

There is a Thinking Stuff from which all things are made, and which, in its original state, permeates, penetrates, and fills the interspaces of the Universe.

A thought, in this substance, produces the thing that is imaged by the thought.

Husband and wife can form things in their thought, and, by impressing their thought upon Formless Substance, can cause the thing they think about to be created.

You must lay aside all other concepts of the Universe than this monistic one; and you must dwell upon this until it is fixed in your mind, and has become your habitual thought. Read these creed statements over and over again; fix every word upon your memory, and meditate upon them until you firmly believe what they say. If a doubt comes to you, cast it aside as a sin. Doubt is the mother of hypocrisy. Do not listen to arguments against this idea;

do not go to churches or lectures where a contrary concept of things is taught or preached. Do not read magazines, books, watch T.V. or visit internet web sites, which teach a different idea; if you get mixed up in your faith, all your efforts will be in vain. Do not take on mixed instructions.

Do not ask why these things are true, nor speculate as to how they can be true; simply take them on trust.

The science of getting rich in marriage begins with the absolute acceptance of this faith.

NOTES

OUR PRINCIPLES ARE THE SPRINGS OF OUR ACTIONS; OUR ACTIONS, THE SPRINGS OF OUR HAPPINESS OR MISERY. TOO MUCH CARE, THEREFORE, CANNOT BE TAKEN IN FORMING OUR PRINCIPLES.
– Philip Skelton

Increasing Ones Marriage

You must get rid of the last vestige of the old idea that there is a Deity whose will it is that you should be poor, or whose purposes may be served by keeping you in poverty.

The Intelligent Substance which is All and in All, and which, lives in All and lives in you, is a consciously Living Substance. Being a consciously living substance, it must have the nature and inherent desire of every living intelligence for increase of life. Every living thing must continually seek for the enlargement of its life, because life, in the mere act of living, must increase itself.

A seed, dropped into the ground, springs into activity, and in the act of living produces a hundred more seeds; life, by living, multiplies itself. It is forever becoming more; it must do so, if it continues to be at all.

Intelligence is under this same necessity for continuous increase. Every thought we think makes it necessary for us to think another thought; consciousness is continually expanding. Every fact we learn leads us to the learning of another fact; knowledge is continually increasing. Every talent we cultivate brings to the mind the desire to cultivate another talent; we are subject to the Urge of Life, seeking expression, which ever drives us on to know more, to do more, and to be more.

In order to know more, do more, and be more we must have more; we must have things to use, for we learn, and do, and become, only by using things. We must get rich, so that we can live more. The desire for riches is simply the capacity for larger life seeking fulfillment; every desire is the effort of an unexpressed possibility to come into action. It is power seeking to manifest which causes desire. That which makes you want more money is the same as that which makes the plant grow; it is Life, seeking fuller expression.

The One Living Substance must be subject to this inherent law of all life; it is permeated with the desire to live more; that is why it is under the necessity of creating things.

The One Substance desires to live more in you; hence, it wants you to have all the things you can use.

It is the desire of God that you should get rich. He wants you to get rich because He can express Himself better through you if you have plenty of things to use in giving Him expression. He can live more in you if you have unlimited command of the means of life.

The Universe desires your marriage to have everything you want to have.

Nature is friendly to your plans in marriage.

Everything is naturally for your marriage.

Make up your mind that this is true.

It is essential, however that your purpose as a couple should harmonize with the purpose that is in All.

You both must want real life, not mere pleasure of sensual gratification. Life is the performance of function; and the individual really lives only when he or she performs every function, physical, mental, and spiritual, of which he or she is capable, without excess in any.

You do not want to get rich in order to live swinishly, for the gratification of animal desires; that is not life. But the performance of every physical function is a part of life, and no one lives completely who denies the impulses of the body a normal and healthful expression. You do not want to get rich solely to enjoy mental pleasures, to get knowledge, to gratify ambition, to outshine others, to be famous. All these are a legitimate part of life, but the man and woman who lives for the pleasures of the intellect alone will only have a partial life, and he or she will never be satisfied with their lot.

You do not want to get rich solely for the good of others, to lose yourself for the salvation of mankind, to experience the joys of philanthropy and sacrifice. The joys of the soul are only a part of life; and they are no better or nobler than any other part.

You want to get rich in order that you may eat, drink, and be merry when it is time to do these things. In order that you may surround yourself with beautiful things, see distant lands, feed your mind, and develop your intellect. In order that you may love people and do kind things, and be able to play a good part in helping the world to find truth.

However, remember that extreme unselfishness is no better and no nobler than extreme selfishness; both are mistakes.

Get rid of the idea that God wants you to sacrifice yourself for others, and that you can secure His favor by doing so; God requires nothing of the kind.

What He wants is that you should make the most of yourself, for yourself, and for others; and you can help others more by making the most of yourself than in any other way.

You can make the most of your marriage only by getting rich; so it is right and praiseworthy that you should give your, first and best thought to the work of acquiring wealth and walking in the pursuit of happiness.

Remember, however, that the desire of Substance is for all, and its movements must be for more life to all; it cannot be made to work for less life to any, because it is equally in all, seeking riches and life.

Intelligent Substance will make things for you; however it will not take things away from someone else and give them to you. You must get rid of the thought of competition. You are to create, not to compete for what is already created.

You do not have to take anything away from any one.

You do not have to drive sharp bargains.

You do not have to cheat, or to take advantage. You do not need to let any man or woman work for you for less than he or she earns.

You do not have to covet the property of others, or to look at it with wishful eyes; no marriage has anything of which you cannot have the like and that without taking what they have away from them.

You are to become creators, not competitors; you are going to get what you want, however in such a way that when you get it every other person will have more than they have now.

We are aware that there are couples who get a vast amount of money by proceeding in direct opposition to the statements in the paragraph above, and may we add a word of explanation here. Men and women of the plutocratic type, who become very rich, do so sometimes purely by their extraordinary ability on the plane of competition; and sometimes they unconsciously relate themselves to Substance in its great purposes and movements for the general racial up building through industrial evolution. Rockefeller, Carnegie, Morgan, et al., have been the unconscious agents of the Supreme in the necessary work of systematizing and organizing productive industry; and in the end, their work will contribute immensely toward increased life for all. Their day is nearly over; they have organized production, and will soon be succeeded by the agents of the multitude, who will organize the machinery of distribution.

The multi-billionaires are like the monster reptiles of the pre-historic eras; they play a necessary part in the evolutionary process, but the same Power which produced them will dispose of them. And it is well to bear in mind that they have never been really rich; a record of the private lives of most of this class will show that they have really been the most abject and wretched of the poor. Riches secured on the competitive plane are never satisfactory and permanent; they are your today, and another's tomorrow. Remember, if you are to become rich in a scientific and Certain Way, you must rise entirely out of the competitive thought. You must never think for a moment that the supply is limited. Just as soon as you begin to think that all the money is being "cornered" and controlled by bankers and others, and thinking that, you must exert yourself to get laws passed to stop this process and so on. In that moment you drop into the competitive mind and your power to cause creation is gone for the time being; and what is worse, you will probably arrest the creative movements you have already instituted.

Know that there is countless trillions of dollars worth of gold in the mountains of the earth, not yet brought to light; and know that if there were not, more would be created from Thinking Substance to supply your needs.

Know that the money you need will come, even if it is necessary for a thousand men to be led to the discovery of new gold mines tomorrow.

Never look at the visible supply; look always at the limitless riches in Formless Substance, and KNOW that they are coming to you as fast as you can receive and use them. Nobody, by cornering the visible supply, can prevent you from getting what is yours.

So never allow yourselves to think for an instant that all the best building spots will be taken before you get ready to build your house, unless you hurry. Never worry about the associations and combines, and get anxious for fear they will soon come to own the whole earth. Never get afraid that you will lose what you want because some other person "beats you to it." That cannot possibly happen; you are not seeking anything that is possessed by anybody else; you are causing what you want to be created from Formless Substance, and the supply is without limits. Stick to the formulated statement:

There is a Thinking Stuff from which all things are made, and which, in its original state, permeates, penetrates, and fills the interspaces of the Universe. A thought, in this substance, produces the thing that is imaged by the thought. Husband and wife can form things in their thought, and, by impressing their thought upon Formless Substance, can cause the things they think about to be created.

NOTES

USE YOUR GIFTS FAITHFULLY, AND THEY SHALL BE ENLARGED; PRACTICE WHAT YOU KNOW, AND YOU SHALL ATTAIN TO HIGHER KNOWLEDGE.

_____
_____
_____
_____
_____
_____
_____
_____
_____
_____
_____
_____
_____
_____
_____
_____
_____
_____
_____
_____
_____

How Riches Come to Your Marriage

When we say that you do not have to drive sharp bargains, we do not mean that you do not have to drive any bargains at all, or that you are above the necessity for having any dealings with your fellow human. We mean that you will not need to deal with people unfairly; you do not have to get something for nothing, however you can give to every man and woman more than you take from him or her. You cannot give, every man and woman more in cash market value than you take from them, but you can give them more in use value than the cash value of the thing you take from them. The paper, ink, and other material in this book may not be worth the money you pay for it; but if the ideas suggested by it bring you more love, happiness, and peace within your marriage, or brings you thousands of dollars, you have not been wronged by those who sold it to you; they have given you a great use value for a small cash value.

Let us suppose that we own a picture by one of the great artists, which, in any civilized community, is worth thousands of dollars. We take it to Peru, and by "salesmanship", we induce an Amahuaca to give a bundle of furs worth $1500 for it. We have really wronged him, for he has no use for the picture; it has no use value to him; it will not add to his life.

But suppose we give him a gun worth $250 for his furs; then he has made a good bargain. He has use for the gun; it will get him many more furs and much food; it will add to his life in every way; it will make him rich.

When you rise from the competitive to the creative plane, you can scan your business transactions very strictly, and if you are selling any person anything, which does not add more to their life than the thing they give you in exchange, you can afford to stop it. You do not have to beat anybody in business. And if you are in a business which does beat people, get out of it at once. Give every person more in use value than you take from them in cash value; then you are adding to the life of the world by every business transaction.

If you have people working for you, you must take from them more in cash value than you pay them in wages; however, you can so organize your business that it will be filled with the principle of advancement, and so that each employee who wishes to do so may advance a little every day.

You can make your business do for your employees what this book is doing for you... You can so conduct your business that it will be a sort of ladder, by which every employee who will take the trouble may climb to riches themselves; and given the opportunity, if they will not do so it is not your fault.

This also goes for your marriage. You both are in the business of serving one another. This is your business. Do not shortchange each other and expect full service from each other.

And finally, because you are to cause the creation of your riches from Formless Substance which permeates all your environment, it does not follow that they are to take shape from the atmosphere and come into being before your eyes.

If you want a car, for instance, we do not mean to tell you that you are to impress the thought of a car on Thinking Substance until the car is formed without hands, outside your home where you sit, or elsewhere. But if you want a car, hold the mental image of it with the most positive certainty that it is being made, or is on its way to you. After once forming the thought, have the most absolute and unquestioning faith that the car is coming; never think of it, or speak, of it, in any other way than as being sure to arrive. Claim it as already yours. This absolutely applies in marriage, hold the image of what it is that you want in your marriage, if it is more affection, see yourself being more affectionate. Form detail thoughts about the marriage that you want to create.

It will be brought to you by the power of the Supreme Intelligence, acting upon your mind and the minds of people. If you live in Washington, it may be that a person will be brought from Chicago or Japan to engage in some transaction, which will result in your getting what you want. If so, the whole matter will be as much to that person's advantage as it is to yours. Do not forget for a moment that the Thinking Substance is through all, in all, communicating with all, and can influence all. The desire of Thinking Substance for fuller life and better living has caused the creation of all the cars already made; and it can cause the creation of millions more, and will, whenever men and women set it in motion by desire and faith, and by acting in a Certain Way.

You can certainly have a loving, peaceful, and enjoyable marriage; and it is just as certain that you can have any other thing or things which you want, and which you will use for the advancement of your own life and the lives of others.

Couples need not hesitate about asking largely, "It is your Father's pleasure to give you the kingdom", said Jesus.

Original Substance wants to live all that is possible in you, and wants you to have all that you can or will use for the living of the most abundant life.

If you fix upon your consciousness the fact that the desire you feel for the possession of riches is one with the desire of Omnipotence for more complete expression, your faith becomes invincible.

Once there was a little boy sitting at a piano, and vainly trying to bring harmony out of the keys he was grieved and provoked by his inability to play real music. When asked the cause of his vexation, he answered, "I can feel the music in me, but I can't make my hands go right". The music in him was the URGE of Original Substance, containing all the possibilities of all life; all that there is of music was seeking expression through the child. God, the One Substance, is trying to live, do and enjoy things through humanity. He is saying, "I want hands to build wonderful structures, to play divine harmonies, to paint glorious pictures; I want feet to run my errands, eyes to see my beauties, tongues to tell mighty truths and to sing marvelous songs," and so on.

All that there is of possibility is seeking expression through men and women. God wants those who can play music to have pianos and every other instrument, and to have the means to cultivate their talents to the fullest extent. He wants those who can appreciate beauty to be able to surround themselves with beautiful things; He wants those who can discern truth to have every opportunity to travel and observe; He wants those who can appreciate dress to be beautifully clothed, and those who can appreciate good food to be luxuriously fed.

He wants all these things because it is Himself that enjoys and appreciates them; it is God who wants to play, and sing, and enjoy beauty, and proclaim truth and wear fine clothes, and eat good foods. "It is God that worketh in you to will and to do," said Paul.

The desire you feel for riches is the Infinite, seeking to express Himself in you as He sought to find expression in the little boy at the piano. The desire you feel for your marriage is the Infinite, seeking to express Himself. There is a newness of every kind in marriage. Moreover, no two marriages are alike. Therefore, you need not hesitate to ask largely. Your part is to focalize and express the desire to God. This is a difficult point with most people; they retain something of the old idea that poverty and self-sacrifice are pleasing to God. They look upon poverty as a part of the plan, a necessity of nature. They have the idea that God has finished His work, and made all that He can make, and that the majority of men and women must stay poor because there is not enough to go around. They hold to so much of this erroneous thought that they feel ashamed to ask for wealth, or more love within their marriages; they try not to want more than a very modest competence, just enough to make them fairly comfortable.

The case of one student who was told that he must get in mind a clear picture of the things he desired, so that the creative thought of them might be impressed on Formless Substance. He was a very poor man, living in a rented house, and having only what he earned from day to day; and he could not grasp the fact that all wealth was his. So, after thinking the matter over, he decided that he might reasonably ask for a new rug for the floor of his best room, and an kerosene stove to heat the house during the cold weather. Following the instructions given in this book, he obtained these things in a few months; and then it dawned upon him that he had not asked enough. He went through the house in which he lived, and planned all the improvements he would like to make in it; he mentally added a bay window here and a room there, until it was complete in his mind as his ideal home; and then he planned its furnishings.

Holding the whole picture in his mind, he began living in the Certain Way, and moving toward what he wanted; and he owns the house now, and is rebuilding it after the form of his mental image. And now, with still larger faith, he is going on to get greater things. It has been unto him according to his faith, and it is so with you and with all of us.

NOTES

THE SADDEST THING THAT CAN BEFALL A SOUL IS
WHEN IT LOSES FAITH IN GOD AND WOMAN.
– Alexander Smith

Gratitude

The illustrations given in the last chapter will have conveyed to the reader the fact that the first step toward getting rich in marriage is to convey the idea of your wants to the Formless Substance.

This is true, and the both of you will see that in order to do so it becomes necessary to relate yourselves to the Formless Intelligence in a harmonious way.

To secure this harmonious relation is a matter of such primary and vital importance that we shall give some space to its discussion here, and give you instructions, which, if you will follow them, will be certain to bring you into perfect unity of mind with God.

The whole process of mental adjustment and atonement can be summed up in one word, gratitude.

First, you believe that there is One Intelligent Substance, from which all things proceed; second, you believe that this Substance gives you everything you desire; and third, you relate yourself to it by a feeling of deep and profound gratitude.

Many couples who order their lives rightly in all other ways are kept in poverty by their lack of gratitude. Having received one gift from God, they cut the wires, which connect them with Him by failing to make acknowledgment.

It is easy to understand that the nearer we live to the source of wealth, the more wealth we shall receive; and it is easy to understand that the soul that is always grateful lives in closer touch with God than the one that never looks to Him in thankful acknowledgment.

The more gratefully we fix our minds on the Supreme when good things come to us, the more good things we will receive, and the more rapidly they will come; and the reason simply is that the mental attitude of gratitude draws the mind into closer touch with the source from which all blessings come.

If it is a new thought to you that gratitude brings your whole mind into closer harmony with the creative energies of the Universe, consider it well, and you will see that it is true. The good things you already have have come to you along the line of obedience to certain laws. Gratitude will lead your mind out along the ways by which things come; and it will keep you in close harmony with creative thought and prevent you from falling into competitive thought.

Gratitude alone can keep you looking toward the All, and prevent you from falling into the error of thinking of the supply as limited; and to do that would be fatal to your hopes.

There is a Law of Gratitude, and it is absolutely necessary that you should observe the law, if you are to get the results you seek.

The Law of Gratitude is the natural principle that action and reaction are always equal, and in opposite directions.

The grateful outreaching of your mind in thankful praise to the Supreme is a liberation or expenditure of force; it cannot fail to reach that to which it addressed, and the reaction is an instantaneous movement towards you.

"Draw nigh unto God, and He will draw nigh unto you." That is a statement of psychological truth.

In addition, if your gratitude is strong and constant, the reaction in Formless Substance will be strong and continuous; the movement of the things you want will be always toward you. Notice the grateful attitude that Jesus took; how He always seems to be saying, "I thank Thee, Father, that Thou hearest me." You cannot exercise much power without gratitude; for it is gratitude that keeps you connected with Power.

However, the value of gratitude does not consist solely in getting you more blessings in the future. Without gratitude, you cannot long keep from dissatisfied thought regarding things as they are.

The moment you permit your mind to dwell with dissatisfaction upon things as they are, you begin to lose ground. You fix attention upon the common, the ordinary, the poor, and the squalid and mean; and your mind takes the form of these things. Then you will transmit these forms or mental images to the Formless and the common, the poor, the squalid, and mean, will come to you and your marriage.

To permit your minds to dwell upon the inferior is to become inferior and to surround yourselves with inferior things.

On the other hand, to fix your attention on the best is to surround yourselves with the best, and to become the best.

The Creative Power within us makes us into the image of that to which we give our attention. We are Thinking Substance, and thinking substance always takes the form of that which it thinks about.

The grateful mind is constantly fixed upon the best; therefore it tends to become the best; it takes the form or character of the best, and will receive the best.

Faith is born of gratitude. The grateful mind continually expects good things, and expectation becomes faith. The reaction of gratitude upon one's own mind produces faith; and every outgoing wave of grateful thanksgiving increases faith. The marriage that has no feeling of gratitude cannot long retain a living faith; and without a living faith you cannot get rich by the creative method, as we shall see in the following chapters.

It is necessary, then, to cultivate the habit of being grateful for every good thing that comes to you; and to give thanks continuously.

And because all things have contributed to the advancement of your marriage, you should include all things in your gratitude.

Do not waste time thinking or talking about the shortcomings or wrong actions of plutocrats or trust magnates. Their organization of the world has made your opportunity; all you get really comes to you because of them.

Do not rage against corrupt politicians; if it were not for politicians we should fall into anarchy, and your opportunity would be greatly lessened.

Do not waste time thinking on the shortcomings of your husband or wife. Realize that the faults you see in each other are for your individual benefit in some way. What better way to manifest your faults openly, then with the one who loves you.

God has worked a long time and very patiently to bring us up to where we are in industry and government and He is going right on with His work. There is not the least doubt that He will do away with plutocrats, trust magnates, captains of industry, and politicians as soon as they can be spared; but in the meantime, behold they are all very good. Remember that they are all helping to arrange the lines of transmission along which your riches will come to you, and be grateful to them all. This will bring your relationship into harmonious relations with the good in everything, and the good in everything will move toward you.

NOTES

*THEY ENJOY MUCH WHO IS THANKFUL FOR LITTLE; A GRATEFUL
MIND IS BOTH A GREAT AND A HAPPY MIND.*
– Thomas Secker

Thinking in the Certain Way

Turn back to the previous chapter and read again the story of the man who formed a mental image of his house, and you will get a fair idea of the initial step toward getting rich and improving, repairing and changing your marriage. As a couple, you both must form a clear and definite mental picture of what you want; you cannot transmit an idea unless you have it yourself.

You must have it before you can give it; and many people fail to impress Thinking Substance because they have themselves only a vague and misty concept of the things they want to do, to have, or to become.

It is not enough that you should have a general desire for wealth "to do good with"; everybody has that desire.

It is not enough that you should have a wish to travel, see things, live more, etc. Everybody has those desires also. If you were going to send a text or email to a friend, you would not send the letters of the alphabet in their order, and let them then construct the message for themselves; nor would you take words at random from the dictionary. You would send a coherent sentence; one which meant something. When you try to impress your wants upon Substance, remember that it must be done by a coherent statement; you both must know what you want, and be definite. You can never get rich, or start the creative power into action, by sending out unformed longings and vague desires.

Go over your desires just as the man we have described went over his house; see just what you want, and get a clear mental picture of it as you wish it to look when you get it. Remember simple things like seeing yourselves holding hands as you sit on the couch watching a movie. Get detailed.

That clear mental picture you must have continually in mind, as the sailor has in mind the port toward which he is sailing the ship; you must keep your face toward it all the time. You must no more lose sight of it than the steersman loses sight of the compass.

It is not necessary to take exercises in concentration, nor to set apart special times for prayer and affirmation, nor to "go into the silence", nor to do occult stunts of any kind. These things are well enough, but all you need is to know what you want, and to want it badly enough so that it will stay in your thoughts.

Spend as much of your leisure time as you can in contemplating your picture, however no one needs to take exercises on how to focus the mind on a thing which you really want; it is the things you do not really care about which require effort to fix your attention upon them.

Furthermore, unless you really want to get rich, so that the desire is strong enough to hold your thoughts directed to the purpose as the magnetic pole holds the needle of the compass, it will hardly be worth your while for you to try to carry out the instructions given in this book.

The methods herein set forth are for couples whose desire for riches is strong enough to overcome mental laziness and the love of ease, and make them work.

The more clear and definite you make your picture then, and the more you both dwell upon it, bringing out all its delightful details, the stronger your desire will be; and the stronger your desire, the easier it will be to hold your minds fixed upon the picture of what you want.

Something more is necessary, however, than merely to see the picture clearly. If that is all you do, you are only a dreamer, and will have little or no power for accomplishment.

Behind your clear vision must be the purpose to realize it; to bring it out in tangible expression.

Behind this purpose must be an invincible and unwavering FAITH that the thing is already yours; that it is "at hand" and you have only to take possession of it.

Live in the new house, mentally, until it takes form around you physically. In the mental realm, enter at once into full enjoyment of the things you want. See your marriage the way you want it now and walk in that expression until it takes form around you.

"Whatsoever things ye ask for when ye pray, believe that ye receive them, and ye shall have them," said Jesus.

See the things you want as if they were actually around you all the time; see yourselves as owning and using them. Make use of them in imagination just as you will use them when they are your tangible possessions. Dwell upon your mental picture until it is clear and distinct, and then take the *Mental Attitude of Ownership* toward everything in that picture. Take possession of it, in mind, in the full faith that it is actually yours. Hold to this mental ownership; do not waiver for an instant in the faith that it is real.

Remember what was said in a proceeding chapter about gratitude; be as thankful for it all the time as you expect to be when it has taken form. The couple, who will sincerely thank God for the things which as of yet they own only in imagination, has real faith. They will get rich; they will cause the creation of whatsoever they want.

You do not need to pray repeatedly for things you want; it is not necessary to tell God about it every day.

"Use not vain repetitions as the heathen do," said Jesus saying to his pupils, "for your Father knoweth what things ye have need of, before ye ask Him."

Your part is to intelligently formulate your desire for the things, which make for a larger life, and to get these desires arranged into a coherent whole; and then to impress this Whole Desire upon the Formless Substance, which has the power and the will to bring you what you want.

You do not make this impression by repeating strings of words; you make it by holding the vision with unshakable PURPOSE to attain it, and with steadfast FAITH that you do attain it.

The answer to prayer is not according to your faith while you are talking, but according to your faith while you are working.

You cannot impress the mind of God by having a special Sabbath day set apart to tell Him what you want, and then forgetting Him during the rest of the week. You cannot impress Him by having special hours to go into your closet and pray, if you then dismiss the matter from your mind until the hour of prayer comes again.

Praying for your marriage only when there is a problem, will not impress upon the Formless Substance your desire for a more abundant marriage.

Oral prayer is well enough, and has its effect, especially upon yourself, in clarifying your vision and strengthening your faith; it is not your oral petitions, which will get you what you want. In order to get rich you do not need a "sweet hour of prayer"; you need to **"Pray without ceasing"** as we are taught in 1Thessalonians 5:17. And by prayer we mean holding steadily to your vision, with the purpose to cause its creation into solid form, and the faith that you are doing so.

"Believe that ye receive them."

The whole matter turns on receiving, once you have clearly formed your vision. When you have formed it, it is well to make an oral statement, addressing the Supreme in reverent prayer; and from that moment you must, in mind, receive what you ask for.

Live in the new house; feel the joy; wear the fine clothes; ride in the automobile of your dreams; have the amazing sex, have time alone; kiss as if it's your first and last kiss; go on the journey and confidently plan for greater journeys. Think and speak of all the things you have asked for in terms of actual present owner-ship. Imagine an environment and all the conditions exactly as you want them, and live all the time in that imaginary environ-ment and financial condition. Mind, however, that you do not do this as a mere dreamer and castle builder; hold to the FAITH that the imaginary is being realized, and to the PURPOSE to realize it. Remember that it is faith and purpose in the use of the imagi-nation, which make the difference between the scientist and the dreamer. In having learned this fact, it is here that you must learn the proper use of the Will.

NOTES

IT IS THE HABITUAL THOUGHT THAT FRAMES ITSELF INTO OUR LIFE. IT AFFECTS US EVEN MORE THAN OUR INTIMATE SOCIAL RELATIONS DO.
– J.W. Teal

How to Use the Will

To set about getting rich in a scientific way, you do not try to apply your will power to anything outside of yourself.

You have no right to do so, anyway.

It is wrong to apply your will to your husband or wife, in order to get them to do what you wish done.

It is as flagrantly wrong to coerce someone by mental power, as it is to coerce someone by physical power. If compelling someone by physical force to do things for you reduces them to slavery, compelling them by mental means accomplishes exactly the same thing; the only difference is in methods. If taking things from someone by physical force is robbery, then taking things by mental force is robbery also; there is no difference in principle.

You have no right to use your will power upon another person including your spouse, even "for their own good"; for you do not know what is "for their own good". The science of getting rich in marriage does not require you to apply power or force to any other person, in any way whatsoever. There is not the slightest necessity for doing so; indeed, any attempt to use your will upon others will only tend to defeat your purpose.

You do not need to apply your will to things, in order to compel them to come to you.

That would simply be trying to coerce God, and would be foolish and useless, as well as IRREVERENT.

You do not have to COMPEL God to give you good things, any more than you have to use your will power to make the sun rise. You do not have to use your will power to conquer an unfriendly deity, or to make stubborn and rebellious forces do your bidding.

Substance is friendly to you, and is more anxious to give you what you want than you are to get it.

To get rich in marriage, you need only to use your will power upon yourself not on one another.

When you know what to think and do, then you must use your will to compel yourselves to think and do the right things. That is the legitimate use of the will in getting what you want to use it in holding yourselves to the right course. Use your will to keep yourselves thinking and acting in the Certain Way.

Do not try to project your will, or your thoughts, or your mind out into space, to "act" on things or people.

Keep your mind at home; it can accomplish more there than elsewhere.

Use your minds to form a mental image of what you both want, and to hold that vision with faith and purpose; and use your will to keep your minds working in the Right Way.

The more steady and continuous your faith and purpose, the more rapidly you will get rich, because you will make only POSITIVE impressions upon Substance; and you will not neutralize or offset them by negative impressions.

The picture of your desires, held with faith and purpose, is taken up by the Formless, and permeates it to great distances throughout the Universe, for all we know.

As this impression spreads, all things are set moving toward its realization; every living thing, every inanimate thing, and the things yet uncreated, are stirred toward bringing into being that which you want. All force begins to be exerted in that direction; all things begin to move toward you. The minds of people, everywhere, are influenced toward doing the things necessary to the fulfilling of your desires; and they work for you, unconsciously.

However, you can check all this by starting a negative impression in the Formless Substance. Doubt or unbelief is as certain to start a movement away from you as faith and purpose are to start one toward you. Doubt is the mother of hypocrisy. It is by not understanding this that most people who try to make use of "mental science" in getting rich in marriage make their failure. Every hour and moment, you spend in giving heed to doubts and fears, every hour you spend in worry, every hour in which your soul is possessed by unbelief, sets a current away from you in the whole domain of Intelligent Substance. All the promises are unto them that believe and unto them only. *"Therefore I say unto you, What things so ever ye desire, when ye pray, believe that ye receive them, and ye shall have them"*. Notice how insistent Jesus was upon this point of belief; and now you know the reason why.

Since belief is **all-important**, it behooves you to guard your thoughts; and as your beliefs will be shaped to a very great extent by the things you observe and think about, it is important that you should command your attention.

This is where the Will comes into use; for it is by your will that you determine upon what things your attention shall be fixed.

If you want to become rich, you must not make a study of poverty. If you want fidelity in your marriage, you must not make a study of infidelity.

Things are not brought into being by thinking about their opposites. Health is never to be attained by studying disease and thinking about disease; righteousness is not to be promoted by studying sin and thinking about sin; and no one ever got rich by studying poverty and thinking about poverty.

Medicine as a science of disease has increased disease; religion as a science of sin has promoted sin, marriage as a science of divorce has increased divorce and economics as a study of poverty will fill the world with wretchedness and want.

Do not talk about poverty; do not investigate it, or concern yourself with it. Do not talk about divorce; do not investigate it, or concern yourselves with it. Never mind what its causes are; you have nothing to do with them. What concerns you is the cure.

Do not spend your time in charitable work, or charity movements; all charity only tends to perpetuate the wretchedness it aims to eradicate.

We are not saying that you should be hardhearted or unkind, and refuse to hear the cry of need; but you must not try to eradicate poverty in any of the conventional ways. Put poverty behind you, and put all that pertains to it behind you, and "make good".

Improve your own marriage; that is the best way you can help other couples and help eliminate divorce.

You cannot hold the mental image, which is to make you rich in marriage, if you fill your minds with pictures of divorce and despair. Do not read books or websites, which give circumstantial accounts of break-ups. Do not fill your minds with any gloomy images of divorce and separation.

There is no way you as a couple can hold the mental image, which is to make you rich, if you fill your minds with pictures of poverty. Do not read books or papers, which give circumstantial accounts of the wretchedness of the tenement dwellers, of the horrors of child labor, and so on. Do not read anything, which fills your mind with gloomy images of want and suffering.

You cannot help the poor in the least by knowing about these things; and the widespread knowledge of them does not tend at all to do away with poverty.

What tends to do away with poverty is not the getting of pictures of poverty into your mind, but getting pictures of wealth into the minds of the poor.

You are not deserting the poor in their misery when you refuse to allow your mind to be filled with pictures of that misery. Poverty can be done away with, not by increasing the number of well to do people who think about poverty, but by increasing the number of poor people who purpose with faith to get rich.

The poor do not need charity; they need inspiration. Charity only sends them a loaf of bread to keep them alive in their wretchedness, or gives them an entertainment to make them forget for an hour or two; but inspiration will cause them to rise out of their misery. If you want to help the poor, demonstrate to them that they can become rich; prove it by getting rich yourself.

The only way in which poverty will ever be banished from this world is by getting a large and constantly increasing number of people to practice the teachings of this book.

People must be taught to become rich by creation, not by competition.

Every man or woman who become rich by competition throws down behind them the ladder by which they rise, and keeps others down; but every man and woman who get rich by creation opens a way for thousands to follow them, and inspires them to do so.

You are not showing hardness of heart or an unfeeling disposition when you refuse to pity poverty, see poverty, read about poverty, or think or talk about it, or to listen to those who do talk about it. Use your will power to keep your mind off the subject of poverty, and to keep it fixed with faith and purpose on the vision of what you want.

NOTES

*TO WILL WHAT GOD WILLS IS THE ONLY
SCIENCE THAT GIVE US REST.*
– Henry Wadsworth Longfellow

Further Use of the Will

You cannot retain a true and clear vision of love, peace, and wealth if you are constantly turning your attention to opposing pictures, whether they be external or imaginary.

Do not tell of your past troubles of any nature, if you have had them, do not think of them at all. Do not tell of the troubles of your parents, or the hardships of your early married life or other past relationships; to do any of these things is to mentally class yourself with the opposite of what you want for the time being, and it will certainly check the movement of things in your direction.

"Let the dead bury their dead", as Jesus said.

Put poverty and all things that pertain to poverty completely behind you.

You have accepted a certain theory of the Universe as being correct, and are resting all your hopes of happiness on its being correct; and what can you gain by giving heed to conflicting theories?

Do not read religious books which tell you that the world is soon coming to an end; and do not read the writing of muckrakers and pessimistic philosophers who tell you that it is going to the devil.

The world is not going to the devil; it is going to God.
It is a wonderful Becoming.

True, there may be a good many things in existing conditions, which are disagreeable; but what is the use of studying them when they are certainly passing away, and when the study of them only tends to check their passing and keep them with us? Why give time and attention to things, which are being removed by evolutionary growth, when you can hasten their removal only by promoting the evolutionary growth as far as your part of it goes?

No matter how horrible in seeming may be the conditions in certain countries, sections, or places, you waste your time and destroy your own chances by considering them. You should interest yourself in the world's becoming rich.

Think of the riches the world is coming into, instead of the poverty it is growing out of; and bear in mind that the only way in which you can assist the world in growing rich is by growing rich yourself through the creative method not the competitive one.

Think of the goodness coming to your marriage, instead of the pain that is passing away. And know that the only way you can help the world is to first improve your own marriage.

Give your attention wholly to riches; ignore the idea of poverty.

Whenever you think or speak of those who are poor, think and speak of them as those who are becoming rich; as those who are to be congratulated rather than pitied. Then they and others will catch the inspiration, and begin to search for the way out.

Because we say that you are to give your whole time and mind and thought to riches, it does not follow that you are to be sordid or mean.

To become really rich is the noblest aim you can have in life and marriage, for it includes everything else. On the competitive plane, the struggle to get rich is a Godless scramble for power over others; but when we come into the creative mind, all this is changed.

All that is possible in the way of greatness and soul unfoldment, of service and lofty endeavor, comes by way of getting rich; all is made possible by the use of things.

If you lack for physical health, you will find that the attainment of it is conditional on your getting rich. Only those who are emancipated from financial worry, and who have the means to live a carefree existence and follow hygienic practices, can have and retain health.

Moral and spiritual greatness is possible only to those who are above the competitive battle for existence; and only those who are becoming rich on the plane of creative thought are free from the degrading influences of competition. *If your heart is set on domestic happiness, remember that love flourishes best where there is refinement, a high level of thought, and freedom from corrupting influences; and these are to be found only where riches are attained by the exercise of creative thought, without strife or rivalry.*

You can aim at nothing so great or noble, we repeat, as to become rich in your marriage; and you must fix your attention upon your mental picture of riches, to the exclusion of all that may tend to dim or obscure the vision.

You must learn to see the underlying TRUTH in all things; you must see beneath all seemingly wrong conditions the Great One Life ever moving forward toward a fuller expression and a more complete happiness.

It is the truth that there is no such thing as poverty; that there is only wealth.

Some couples remain in poverty because they are ignorant of the fact that there is wealth for them; and these can best be taught by showing them the way to affluence in your own person, marriage, and practice.

Others are poor because, while they feel that there is a way out, they are too intellectually lazy to put forth the mental effort necessary to find the way and to travel it; and for these the very best thing you can do is to arouse their desire by showing them the happiness that comes from being rightly rich.

Others still are poor because, while they have some notion of science, they have become so swamped and lost in the maze of metaphysical and occult theories that they do not know which road to take. They try a mixture of many systems and fail in all. For these, again, the very best thing, to do is to show the right way in your own person, marriage, and practice; an ounce of doing things is worth a pound of theorizing.

The very best thing you can do for the whole world is to make the most of yourself and your marriage.

You can serve God and man in no more effective way than by getting rich; that is, if you get rich by the creative method and not by the competitive one. The better our marriages are the better the environments are for our families and we create a cycle of goodness.

In addition to the above statements, we assert that this book gives in detail the principles of the science of getting rich in marriage; and if that is true, you do not need to read any other book upon the subject. This may sound narrow and egotistical, but think on this. There is no more scientific method of computation in mathematics than by addition, subtraction, multiplication, and division; no other method is possible. There can be but one shortest distance between two points. There is only one-way to think scientifically, and that is to think in the way that leads by the most direct and simple route to the goal. No man or woman has yet formulated a briefer or less complex "system" than the one set forth herein; it has been stripped of all non-essentials. When you commence on this, lay all others aside; put them out of your mind altogether.

Read this book every day; keep it with you; read it together; commit it to memory, and do not think about other "systems" and theories. If you do, you will begin to have doubts and to be uncertain and wavering in your thought; and then you will begin to make failures.

After you have made good and become rich, you may study other systems as much as you please; but until you are quite sure that you have gained what you want, do not read anything on this line but this book, unless it be the authors mentioned in the preface.

And read only the most optimistic comments on the world's news; those in harmony with your picture. Also, postpone your investigations into the occult. Do not dabble in theosophy, spiritualism, or kindred studies. It is very likely that the dead still live, and are near; but if they are, let them alone; mind your own business.

Wherever the spirits of the dead may be, they have their own work to do, and their own problems to solve; and we have no right to interfere with them. We cannot help them, and it is very doubtful whether they can help us, or whether we have any right to trespass upon their time if they can. Let the dead and the hereafter alone, and solve your own problem; get rich. If you begin to mix with the occult, you will start mental cross currents, which will surely bring your hopes to shipwreck. Now, this and the preceding chapters have brought us to the following statement of basic facts.

There is a Thinking Stuff from which all things are made, and which, in its original state, permeates, penetrates, and fills the interspaces of the Universe. A thought, in this substance, produces the thing that is imaged by the thought. Husband and wife can form things in their thought, and, by impressing their thought upon Formless Substance, can cause the thing they think about to be created.

In order to do this, husband and wife must pass from the competitive to the creative mind; they must form a clear mental picture of the thing they want, and hold this picture in their thoughts with the fixed PURPOSE to get what they want, and the unwavering FAITH that they do get what they want, closing their mind against all that may tend to shake their purpose, dim their vision, or quench their faith.

In addition to all this, we shall now see that you must live and act in a Certain Way.

NOTES

PEOPLE DO NOT LACK STRENGTH; THEY LACK WILL.
— Victor Hugo

Acting in the Certain Way

Thought is the creative power, or the impelling force, which causes the creative power to act; thinking in a Certain Way will bring riches to your marriage, however you must not rely upon thought alone, paying no attention to personal action. This is the rock upon which many otherwise scientific metaphysical thinkers meet shipwreck. The failure to connect thought with personal action.

We have not yet reached the stage of development, even supposing such a stage to be possible, in which we can create directly from Formless Substance without nature's processes or the work of human hands; we must not only think, however personal action must supplement our thought.

By thought, you can cause the gold in the hearts of the mountains to be impelled toward you; however, it will not mine itself, refine itself, coin itself into double eagles, and come rolling along the streets seeking its way into your pocket.

Under the impelling power of the Supreme Spirit, men and women's affairs will be so ordered that someone will be led to mine the gold for you. Other business transactions will be so directed that the gold will be brought toward you, and you must so arrange your own business affairs that you may be able to receive it when it comes to you. Your thought makes all things, animate and inanimate, work to bring you what you want; your personal activity must be such that you as a couple can rightly receive what you want when it reaches you. You are not to take it as charity, nor to steal it; you must give every man, woman and child more in use value than they give you in cash value.

The scientific use of thought consists in forming a clear and distinct mental image of what you want; in holding fast to the purpose to get what you want; and in realizing with grateful faith that you do get what you want.

Do not try to "project" your thought in any mysterious or occult way, with the idea of having it go out and do things for you; that is wasted effort, and will weaken your power to think with sanity.

The action of thought in getting rich in marriage we fully explain in the preceding chapters; your faith and purpose positively impress your vision upon Formless Substance, which has THE SAME DESIRE FOR MORE LIFE THAT YOU HAVE.

This vision, received from you, sets all the creative forces at work IN AND THROUGH THEIR REGULAR CHANNELS OF ACTION, however directed towards your marriage.

It is not your part to guide or supervise the creative process; all you have to do with that is to retain your vision, stick to your purpose, and maintain your faith and gratitude.

However, you must act in a Certain Way, so that you can appropriate what is yours when it comes to you; so that you can meet the things you have in your picture, and put them in their proper places as they arrive.

You can really see the truth of this. When things reach you, they will be in the hands of other men or women, who will ask an equivalent for them.

Understand that you can only get what is yours by giving the other person what is theirs.

Your pocketbook is not going to be transformed into a Fortunata's purse, which shall be always full of money without effort on your part.

This is the crucial point in the science of getting rich in marriage; right here, where *thought and personal action must be combined.* There are very many who, consciously or unconsciously, set the creative forces in action by the strength and persistence of their desires, however, who remain poor because they do not provide for the reception of the thing they want when it comes. *By thought, the thing you want is brought to you; by action, you receive it.*

Whatever your action is to be, it is evident that you must act NOW. You cannot act in the past, and it is essential to the clearness of your mental vision that you dismiss the past from your mind. You cannot act in the future, for the future is not here yet and you cannot tell how you will want to act in any future contingency until that contingency has arrived.

Because you are not in the right business, or the right environment now, do not think that you must postpone action until you get into the right business or environment. And do not spend time in the present taking thought as to the best course in possible future emergencies; have faith in your ability to meet any emergency when it arrives.

If you act in the present with your mind on the future, your present action will be with a divided mind, and will not be effective.

Put your whole mind into present action.

Do not give your creative impulse to Original Substance, and then sit down and wait for results; if you do, you will never get them. Act now. There is never any time but now, and there never will be any time but now. If you are ever to begin to make ready for the reception of what you want, you must begin now.

Know and understand that your action, whatever it is, must most likely be in your present business or employment, and must be upon the persons and things in your present environment.

You cannot act where you are not; you cannot act where you have been, and you cannot act where you are going to be; you can act only where you are.

Do not bother as to whether yesterday's work was well done or ill done; do to-day's work well. Do not try to do tomorrow's work now; there will be plenty of time to do that when you get to it.

Do not try, by occult or mystical means, to act on people or things that are out of your reach.

*Do not wait for a change of environment, before you act,
get a change of environment by action.*

You can so act upon the environment in which you are now, as to cause yourself to be transferred to a better environment.

Hold with faith and purpose the vision of yourselves in a better environment; however act upon your present environment with all your heart, and with all your strength, and with your entire mind.

Do not spend any time in daydreaming or castle building; hold to the one vision of what you want, and act NOW.

Do not cast about seeking some new thing to do, or some strange, unusual, or remarkable action to perform as a first step toward getting rich. It is probable that your actions, at least for some time to come, will be those you have been performing for some time past; but you are to begin now to perform these actions in the Certain Way, which will surely make you rich.

If you are engaged in some business, and feel that it is not the right one for you, do not wait until you get into the right business before you begin to act.

Do not feel discouraged, or sit down and lament because you are misplaced. No man or woman was ever so misplaced that he or she could not find the right place, and no man or woman has ever became so involved in the wrong business that he or she could not get into the right business.

Hold the vision of yourselves in the right business, with the purpose to get into it, and the faith that you will get into it, and are getting into it; but ACT in your present business. Use your present business as the means of getting a better one, and use your present environment as the means of getting into a better one. Your vision of the right business, if held with faith and purpose, will cause the Supreme to move the right business toward you; and your action, if performed in the Certain Way, will cause you to move toward the business.

If you are an employee, or wage earner, and feel that you must change places in order to get what you want, do not "project" your thought into space and rely upon it to get you another job. It will probably fail to do so.

Hold the vision of yourselves in the job you want, while you ACT with faith and purpose on the job you have, and you will certainly get the job you want.

Your vision and faith will set the creative force in motion to bring it toward you, and your action will cause the forces in your own environment to move you toward the place you want. In closing this chapter, we will add another statement to our syllabus:

There is a Thinking Stuff from which all things are made, and which, in its original state, permeates, penetrates, and fills the interspaces of the Universe.

A thought, in this substance, produces the thing that is imaged by the thought.

Husband and wife can form things in their thought, and, by impressing their thought upon Formless Substance, can cause the thing they think about to be created.

In order to do this, husband and wife must pass from the competitive to the creative mind; they must form a clear mental picture of the things they want, and hold this picture in their thoughts with the fixed PURPOSE to get what they want, and the unwavering FAITH that they do get what they want, closing their minds to all that may tend to shake their purpose, dim their vision, or quench their faith.

That they may receive what they want when it comes, husband and wife must act NOW upon the people and things in their present environment.

NOTES

*HEAVEN NEVER HELPS THE MAN AND
WOMAN WHO WILL NOT ACT*
– Sophocles

Efficient Action

You must use your thought as directed in previous chapters, and begin to do what you can do where you are; and you must do ALL that you can do where you are.

You can advance only by being larger than your present place; and no marriage is larger than its present place who leaves undone any of the work pertaining to that place.

The world is advanced only by those who more than fill their present places.

If no man or woman quite filled his or her present place, you can see that there must be a going backward in everything. Those who do not quite fill their present places are dead weight upon society, government, commerce, and industry. Others must carry them along at a great expense. Only those who do not fill the places they are holding retard the progress of the world; they belong to a former age and a lower stage or plane of life, and their tendency is toward degeneration. No society could advance if every man and woman were smaller than his or her place; the law of physical and mental evolution guides social evolution. In the animal world, evolution is caused by excess of life.

When an organism has more life than can be expressed in the functions of its own plane, it develops the organs of a higher plane, and a new species is originated.

There never would have been new species had there not been organisms, which more than filled their places. The law is exactly the same for you; your getting rich in marriage depends upon your applying this principle to your own affairs.

Every day is either a successful day or a day of failure; and it is the successful days, which get you what you want. If every day is a failure, you can never get rich. While if every day is a success, you cannot fail to get rich.

If there is something that may be done today, and you do not do it, you have failed in so far as that thing is concerned; and the consequences may be more disastrous than you imagine.

You cannot foresee the results of even the most trivial act; you do not know the workings of all the forces that have been set moving on your behalf. Much may be depending on your doing some simple act; it may be the very thing, which is to open the door of opportunity to very great possibilities. You can never know all the combinations which the Supreme Intelligence is making for you in the world of things and of things and of human affairs; your neglect or failure to do some small thing may cause a long delay in getting what you want.

Do, every day, ALL that can be done that day.

There is, however, a limitation or qualification of the above that you must take into account.

You are not to overwork, nor to rush blindly into your business in the effort to do the greatest possible number of things in the shortest possible time.

You are not to try to do tomorrow's work today, nor to do a week's work in a day.

It is really not the number of things you do, but the EFFICIENCY of each separate action that counts.

Every act is, in itself, either a success or a failure.

Every act is, in itself, either effective or inefficient.

Every inefficient act is a failure, and if you spend your life doing inefficient acts, your whole life will be a failure.

The more inefficient things you do, the worse for you, if all your acts are inefficient ones.

On the other hand, every efficient act is a success in itself, and if every act of your life is an efficient one, your whole life, and marriage MUST be a success.

The cause of failure is doing too many things in an inefficient manner, and not doing enough things in an efficient manner.

You will see that it is a self-evident proposition that if you do not do any inefficient acts, and if you do a sufficient number of efficient acts, you will become rich. If it is possible for you to make each act an efficient one, you see again that the getting of riches is reduced to an exact science, like mathematics.

The matter turns, then, on the questions whether you can make each separate act a success in itself. This you both can certainly do.

You can make each act a success, because ALL Power is working with you; and ALL Power cannot fail.

Power is at your service; and to make each act efficient you have only to put power into it.

And your Lord says: "Pray to Me, I will answer you. Those who disdain My service will surely enter hell, abased."

Every action is either strong or weak; and when every action is strong, you are acting in the Certain Way which will make you rich.

Every act can be made strong and efficient by holding your vision while you are doing it, and putting the whole power of your FAITH and PURPOSE into it.

It is at this point that the people fail who separate mental power from personal action. They use the power of mind in one place and at one time, and they act in another place and at another time. Therefore, their acts are not successful in themselves; too many of them are inefficient. Nevertheless, if ALL Power goes into every act, no matter how commonplace, every act will be a success in itself; and as in the nature of things every success opens the way to other successes, your progress toward what you want, and the progress of what you want toward you, will become increasingly rapid.

Remember that successful action is cumulative in its results. Since the desire for more life is inherent in all things, when a couple begins to move toward larger life more things attach themselves to them, and the influence of their desire is multiplied.

Do, every day, all that you can do that day, and do each act in an efficient manner.

In saying that you must hold your vision while you are doing each act, however trivial or commonplace, we do not mean to say that it is necessary at all times to see the vision distinctly to its smallest details. It should be the work of your leisure hours to use your imagination on the details of your vision, and to contemplate them until they are firmly fixed upon your memory. If you wish speedy results, spend practically all your spare time in this practice.

By continuous contemplation you will get the picture of what it is that both of you want, even to the smallest details, so firmly fixed upon your minds, and so completely transferred to the mind of Formless Substance. When in your working hours you need only to mentally refer to the picture to stimulate your faith and purpose, and cause your best effort to be put forth. Contemplate your picture in your leisure hours until your consciousness is so full of it that you can grasp it instantly. You will become so inspired with its bright promises that the mere thought of it will call forth the strongest energies of your whole being.

Let us again repeat our syllabus, and by slightly changing the closing statements bring it to the point that we have now reached.

There is a Thinking Stuff from which all things are made, and which, in its original state, permeates, penetrates, and fills the interspaces of the Universe.

A thought, in this substance, produces the thing that is imaged by the thought.

Husband and wife can form things in their thought and by impressing their thought upon Formless Substance, can cause the thing they think about to be created.

In order to do this, husband and wife must pass from the competitive to the creative mind; they must form a clear mental picture of the thing they want, and do, with faith and purpose, all that can be done each day, doing each separate thing in an efficient manner.

NOTES

A RIGHT ACT STRIKES A CHORD THAT EXTENDS THROUGH THE WHOLE UNIVERSE, TOUCHES ALL MORAL INTELLIGENCE, VISITS EVERY WORLD, VIBRATES ALONG ITS WHOLE EXTENT, AND CONVEYS ITS VIBRATIONS TO THE VERY BOSOM OF GOD!
– Thomas Binney

Getting into the Right Business

Success, in any particular business, depends for one thing upon your possessing in a well-developed state the faculties required in that business.

Without good musical faculty, no one can succeed as a teacher of music; without well-developed mechanical faculties, no one can achieve great success in any of the mechanical trades; without tact and the commercial faculties, no one can succeed in mercantile pursuits. Nevertheless, to possess in a well-developed state the faculties required in your particular vocation does not insure getting rich. There are musicians who have remarkable talent, and who yet remain poor; there are blacksmiths, carpenters, and so on who have excellent mechanical ability, but who do not get rich; and there are merchants with good faculties for dealing with men who nevertheless fail.

The different faculties are tools; it is essential to have good tools, however it is also essential that the tools should be used in the Right Way. A man or woman can take a sharp saw, a square, a good plane, and so on, and build a handsome article of furniture; another man or woman can take the same tools and set to work to duplicate the article, but their production will be a botch. They do not know how to use good tools in a successful way.

The various faculties of your mind are the tools with which you must do the work, which is to make you rich; it will be easier for you to succeed if you get into a business for which you are well equipped with mental tools.

Generally speaking, you will do best in that business which will use your strongest faculties; the one for which you are naturally "best fitted." However, there are limitations to this statement, also.

No man or woman should regard their vocation as being irrevocably fixed by the tendencies with which they were born.

You can get rich in ANY business, for if you have not the right talent for you can develop that talent; it merely means that you will have to make your tools as you go along, instead of confining yourself to the use of those with which you were born. It will be EASIER for you to succeed in a vocation for which you already have the talents in a well-developed state; however, you CAN succeed in any vocation, for you can develop any rudimentary talent, and there is no talent of which you have not at least the rudiment.

You will get rich most easily in point of effort, if you do that for which you are best fitted; but you will get rich most satisfactorily if you do that which you WANT to do.

Doing what you want to do is Life; and there is no real satisfaction in living if we are compelled to be forever doing something, which we do not like to do, and can never, do what we want to do. And it is certain that you can do what you want to do; the desire to do it is proof that you have within you and your marriage the power which can do it.

Desire is a manifestation of power.

The desire to play music is the power, which can play music seeking expression and development; the desire to invent mechanical devices is the mechanical talent seeking expression and development.

Where there is no power, either developed or undeveloped, to do a thing, there is never any desire to do that thing; and where there is strong desire to do a thing, it is certain proof that the power to do it is strong, and only requires to be developed and applied in the Right Way.

All things else being equal, it is best to select the business for which you have the best-developed talent; however if you have a strong desire to engage in any particular line of work, you should select that work as the ultimate end at which you aim. You can do what you want to do, and it is your right and privilege to follow the business or vocation, which will be most congenial and pleasant.

You are not obliged to do what you do not like to do, and should not do it except as a means to bring you to the doing of the thing you want to do.

If there are past mistakes, whose consequences have placed you in an undesirable business or environment. You may be obliged for some time to do what you do not like to do; *you can make the doing of it pleasant by knowing that it is making it possible for you to come to the doing of what you want to do.*

If you feel that you are not in the right vocation, do not act too hastily in trying to get into another one. The best way, generally, to change business or environment is by growth.

Do not be afraid to make a sudden and radical change if the opportunity is presented, and you feel after careful consideration that it is the right opportunity; never take sudden or radical action when you are in doubt as to the wisdom of doing so.

There is never any hurry on the creative plane; and there is *no lack of opportunity.*

When you get out of the competitive mind you will understand that you never need to ACT HASTILY. No one else is going to beat you to the thing you want to do; there is enough for all. If one space is taken, another and a better one will be opened for you a little farther on; there is plenty of time. When you are in doubt, wait. Fall back on the contemplation of your vision, and increase your faith and purpose; and by all means, in times of doubt and indecision, cultivate gratitude.

A day or two spent in contemplating the vision of what you want, and in earnest thanksgiving that you are getting it, will bring your mind into such close relationship with the Supreme that you will make no mistake when you do act. There is a Mind which knows all there is to know; and you can come into close unity with this Mind by faith and the purpose to advance in life, if you have deep gratitude.

Mistakes come from acting hastily, or from acting in fear or doubt, or in forgetfulness of the **right motive**, which is more life to all, and less to none.

As you go on in the Certain Way, opportunities will come to you in increasing number; and you will need to be very steady in your faith and purpose, and to keep in close touch with the All Mind by reverent gratitude.

Do all that you can do in a perfect manner every day, and do it without haste, worry, or fear. Go as fast as you can, never hurry.

Remember that in the moment you begin to hurry you cease to be a creator and become a competitor; you drop back upon the old plane again.

Whenever you find yourselves hurrying, call a halt; fix your attention on the mental image of the thing you want, and begin to give thanks that you are getting it. The exercise of GRATITUDE will never fail to strengthen your faith and renew your purpose.

NOTES

*SUCCESS OR FAILURE IN BUSINESS IS CAUSED MORE BY THE
MENTAL ATTITUDE EVEN THAN BY MENTAL CAPACITIES.*
— *Walter Dill Scott*

The Impression of Increase

Whether you change your vocation or not, your actions for the present must be those pertaining to the business in which you are now engaged.

You can get into the business you want by making constructive use of the business you are already established in; by doing your daily work in a Certain Way.

Moreover, in so far as your business consists in dealing with other men and women, whether personally or by letter, the key-thought of all your efforts must be to convey to their minds the impression of increase.

Increase is what all men and all women are seeking; it is the Urge of the Formless Intelligence within them, seeking fuller expression.

The desire for increase is inherent in all nature; it is the fundamental impulse of the Universe. All human activities are based on the desire for increase; people are seeking more food, more clothes, better shelter, more luxury, more beauty, more knowledge, more pleasure increase in something, more life.

Every living thing is under this necessity for continuous advancement; where increase of life ceases, dissolution and death set in at once.

Man and woman instinctively know this, and hence they are forever seeking more. Jesus sets this law of perpetual increase forth in the parable of the talents; only those who gain more retain any. "For unto every one that hath shall be given, and he shall have abundance: but from him that hath not shall be taken away even that which he hath."

The normal desire for increased wealth is not an evil or a reprehensible thing; it is simply the desire for more abundant life; it is aspiration and because it is the deepest instinct of their natures, all men and women are attracted to those who can give them more of the means of life.

In following the Certain Way as described in the foregoing pages, you are getting continuous increase for yourselves, and you are giving it to all with whom you deal.

You are creative centers, from which increase is given off to all.

Be sure of this, and convey assurance of the fact to every man, woman, and child with whom you come in contact. No matter how small the transaction, even if it be only the selling of a newspaper to a passerby, put into it the thought of increase, and make sure that the customer is impressed with the thought.

Convey the impression of advancement with everything you do, so that all people shall receive the impression that you are an Advancing Couple, and that you advance all who deal with you. Even to the people whom you meet in a social way, without any thought of business, and to whom you do not try to sell anything, give the thought of increase.

You can convey this impression by holding the unshakable faith that you, as a couple, are in the Way of Increase; and by letting this faith inspire, fill, and permeate every action.

Do everything that you do in the firm conviction that you are advancing personalities, and that you are giving advancement to everybody.

Feel that you are getting rich, and that in so doing you are making others rich, and conferring benefits on all.

Do not boast or brag of your success, or talk about it unnecessarily; true faith is never boastful.

Wherever you find a boastful person, you find one who is secretly doubtful and afraid. Simply feel the faith, and let it work out in every transaction; let every act and tone and look express the quiet assurance that you are getting rich; that you are already rich.

Words will not be necessary to communicate this feeling to others; they will feel the sense of increase when in your presence, and will be attracted to you again.

You must so impress others that they will feel that in associating with you they will get increase for themselves. See that you give them a use value greater than the cash value you are taking from them.

Take an honest pride in doing this, and let everybody know it; and you will have no lack of customers. People will go where they are given increase; and the Supreme, which desires increase in all, and which knows all, will move toward you men and women who have never heard of you. Your business will increase rapidly, and you will be surprised at the unexpected benefits, which will come to you. You will be able from day to day to make larger combinations, secure greater advantages, and to go on into a more congenial vocation if you desire to do so.

However, in doing all this, you must never lose sight of your VISION; of what it is you want, your FAITH, and PURPOSE to get what you want.

Let us here give you another word of caution in regard to motives.

Beware of the insidious temptation to seek for
power over your spouse and others.

Nothing is as pleasant to the unformed or partially developed mind as the exercise of power or dominion over others. The desire to rule for selfish gratification has been the curse of the world. For countless ages, kings, rulers, and lords have drenched the earth with blood in their battles to extend their dominions; this is not to seek more life for all, but to get more power for themselves.

Today, the main motive in the business and industrial world is the same; men and women marshal their armies of dollars, and lay waste the lives and hearts of millions in the same mad scramble for power over others. Commercial kings, political kings, and religious kings are inspired by the lust for power.

Jesus saw in this desire for mastery over people. The moving impulse of that evil world He sought to overthrow. Read the twenty-third chapter of Matthew, and see how He pictures the lust of the Pharisees to be called "Master", to sit in the high places, to domineer over others, and to lay burdens on the backs of the less fortunate. Observe how He compares this lust for dominion with the brotherly seeking for the Common Good to which He calls His disciples.

Look out for the temptation to seek for authority, to become a "Master," to be considered as one who is above the common herd, to impress others by lavish display, and so on.

The mind that seeks for mastery over others is the competitive mind; and the competitive mind is not the creative one. In order to master your environment and your destiny, it is not at all necessary that you should rule over your fellow man and indeed, when you fall into the world's struggle for the high places, you begin to be conquered by fate and environment, and your getting rich becomes a matter of chance and speculation.

Beware of the competitive mind! No better statement of the principle of creative action can be formulated than the favorite declaration of the late "Golden Rule" Jones of Toledo: "What we want for ourselves, we want for everybody." What I want for myself, I want for everybody.

NOTES

EVERY HUMAN BEING IS INTENDED TO HAVE A CHARACTER OF THEIR OWN; TO BE WHAT NO OTHER IS, AND TO DO WHAT NO OTHER CAN DO.

The Advancing Marriage

What we have said in the last chapter applies as well to the professional marriage and the wage-earner marriage as to the couple who is engaged in commercial business.

No matter whether you are a physician, a teacher, or a clergyman, if you can give increase of life to others and make them sensible of the fact, they will be attracted to you, and you will get rich. The physicians who hold the vision of themselves as a great and successful healer, and who works toward the complete realization of that vision with faith and purpose, as described in former chapters, will come into such close touch with the Source of Life that they will be phenomenally successful; patients will come to them in throngs.

No one has a greater opportunity to carry into effect the teaching of this book than the practitioner of medicine; it does not matter to which of the various schools he or she may belong, for the principle of healing is common to all of them, and may be reached by all alike. The advancing couple in medicine, who holds to a clear mental image of themselves as successful, and who obeys the laws of faith, purpose, and gratitude, will cure every curable case they undertake, no matter what remedies they may use.

In the field of religion, the world cries out for the clergy who can teach their hearers the true science of abundant life. One who masters the details of the science of getting rich in marriage, together with the allied sciences of being well, of being great, and of winning love, and who teaches these details from the pulpit, will never lack for a congregation. This is the gospel that the world needs; it will give increase of life, and men and women will hear it gladly, and will give liberal support to the one who brings it to them.

What is now needed is a demonstration of the Science of Life from the pulpit. We want preachers, ministers, and rabbis who will not only tell us how, but who in their own persons will show us how. We need the preacher, the minister, the rabbi who will be rich themselves, healthy, great, and beloved, to teach us how to attain to these things; and when they come they will find a numerous and loyal following.

The same is true of the teachers who can inspire the children with the faith and purpose of the advancing life. They will never be "out of a job". In addition, any teacher who has this faith and purpose can give it to their pupils; they cannot help giving it to them if it is part of their own life, marriage, and practice.

What is true of the teacher, preacher, and physician is true of the lawyer, dentist, real estate man, insurance agent and of everybody.

The combined mental and personal action we have described is infallible; it cannot fail. Every man and woman who follow these instructions steadily, perseveringly, and to the letter, will get rich. The law of the Increase of Life is as mathematically certain in its operation as the law of Gravitation; getting rich in marriage is an exact science.

The wage earners will find this as true of their case as of any of the others mentioned. Do not feel that you have no chance to get rich because you are working where there is no visible opportunity for advancement, where wages are small, and the cost of living high. Form your clear mental vision of what you want, and begin to act with faith and purpose.

Do all the work you can do, every day, and do each piece of work in a perfectly successful manner; *put the power of success, and the purpose to get rich, into everything that you do.*

However, do not do this merely with the idea of currying favor with your employer, in the hope that they, or those above you, will see your good work and advance you; it is not likely that they will do so.

The man and woman who is merely a "good" worker, filling their place to the very best of their ability, and satisfied with that, is valuable to their employer; and it is not to the employer's interest to promote them; they are worth more where they are.

To secure advancement, something more is necessary than to be too large for your place.

The one who is certain to advance is the one, who is too big for their place, and who has a clear concept of what they want to be; who knows that they can become what they want to be and who are determined to be what they want to be.

Do not try to more than fill your present place with a view to pleasing your employer; do it with the idea of advancing yourself. Hold the faith and purpose of increase during work hours, after work hours, and before work hours. Hold it in such a way that every person who comes in contact with you, whether foreman, fellow workman, or social acquaintance, will feel the power of purpose radiating from you; so that everyone will get the sense of advancement and increase from you. Men and women will be attracted to you as a couple, and if there is no possibility for advancement in your present jobs, you will very soon see an opportunity to take another job.

There is a *power*, which never fails to present opportunity to the Advancing Marriage who is moving in obedience to law.

God cannot help helping you, if you act in a Certain Way; He must do so in order to help Himself.

There is nothing in your circumstances or in the industrial situation that can keep you down. If you cannot get rich working in the auto industry, you can get rich on the internet; and if you begin to move in the Certain Way, you will certainly escape from the "clutches" of the auto industry and get on to the internet or wherever else you wish to be.

If a few thousands of its employees would enter upon the Certain Way, the auto industry would soon be in a bad plight; it would have to give its workingmen more opportunity, or go out of business.

Nobody has to work for the auto industry; the auto industry can keep men and women in so-called hopeless conditions only so long as there are men and women who are too ignorant to know of the science of getting rich in marriage or too intellectually slothful to practice it.

Begin this way of thinking and acting, and your faith and purpose will make you quick to see any opportunity to better your condition.

Such opportunities will speedily come, for the Supreme, working in all, and working for your marriage, will bring them before you.

Do not wait for an opportunity to be all that you want it to be; when an opportunity to be more than you are now is presented and you feel impelled toward it, take it. It will be the first step toward a greater opportunity.

There is no such thing as the lack of opportunities in this Universe for the men and women who are living the advancing life.

It is inherent in the constitution of the cosmos that all things shall be for him or her and work together for his or her good; and they must certainly get rich if they act and think in the Certain Way. So let wage-earning couple study this book with great care, and enter with confidence upon the course of action it prescribes; it will not fail.

NOTES

SLUMBER NOT IN THE HOMES OF YOUR FATHERS.
THE WORLD IS ADVANCING. ADVANCE WITH IT.

Some Cautions and Concluding Observations

Many people will sneer at the idea that there is an exact science of getting rich in marriage; holding the impression that the supply of wealth is limited, they will insist that social and governmental institutions must be changed before even any considerable number of people can acquire a competence. This is not true.

It is true that existing governments keep the masses in poverty, but this is because the masses do not think and act in the Certain Way.

If the masses begin to move forward as suggested in this book, neither governments nor industrial systems can check them; all systems must be modified to accommodate the forward movement.

If a married couple has the Advancing Mind, the Faith that they can become rich in marriage, and move forward with the fixed purpose to become rich, nothing can possibly keep them in poverty.

Couples may enter upon the Certain Way at any time, and under any government, and make themselves rich; and when any considerable number of couples do so under any government, they will cause the system to be so modified as to open the way for others.

The more men and women who get rich on the competitive plane, the worse for others; the more who get rich on the creative plane, the better for others.

The economic salvation of the masses can only be accomplished by getting a large number of people to practice the scientific method set down in this book, and become rich. These will show others the way, and inspire them with a desire for real life, with the faith that it can be attained, and with the purpose to attain it.

For the present, however, it is enough to know that neither the government under which you live; nor the capitalistic or competitive system of industry can keep you from getting rich. When you enter upon the creative plane of thought, you will rise above all these things and become a citizen of another kingdom.

Remember that your thought must be held upon the creative plane; you are never for an instant to be betrayed into regarding the supply as limited, or into acting on the moral level of competition.

Whenever you do fall into old ways of thought, correct yourselves instantly; for when you are in the competitive mind, you have lost the cooperation of the Mind of the Whole.

Do not spend any time in planning as to how you will meet possible emergencies in the future, except as the necessary policies may affect your actions today. You are concerned with doing today's work in a perfectly successful manner, and not with emergencies, which may arise tomorrow; you can attend to them as they come.

Do not concern yourselves with questions as to how you shall surmount obstacles, which may loom upon your business horizon, unless you can see plainly that your course must be altered today in order to avoid them.

No matter how tremendous an obstruction may appear at a distance, you will find that if you go on in the Certain Way it will disappear as you approach it, or that a way over, through, or around it will appear.

No possible combination of circumstances can defeat a marriage that is proceeding to get rich along strictly scientific lines. No couple who obeys the law can fail to get rich, any more than one can multiply two by two and fail to get four.

Give no anxious thought to possible disasters, obstacles, panics, or unfavorable combinations of circumstances; it is time enough to meet such things when they present themselves before you in the immediate present, and you will find that every difficulty carries with it the wherewithal for its overcoming.

Guard your speech. Never speak of yourselves, your affairs, or of anything else in a discouraged or discouraging way.

Never admit the possibility of failure, or speak in a way that infers failure as a possibility.

Never speak of the times as being hard, or of business conditions as being doubtful. Times may be hard and business doubtful for those who are on the competitive plane, but they can never be so for you; you can create what you want, and you are above fear.

When others are having hard times and poor business, you will find your greatest opportunities.

Train yourselves to think of and to look upon the world as a something, which is becoming, which is growing; and to regard seeming evil as being only that, which is undeveloped. Always speak in terms of advancement; to do otherwise is to deny your faith, and to deny your faith is to lose it.

Never allow yourselves to feel disappointed. You may expect to have a certain thing at a certain time, and not get it at that time; and this will appear to you like failure.

If you hold to your faith, you will find that the failure is only apparent.

Go on in the Certain Way, and if you do not receive that thing, you will receive something so much better that you will see that the seeming failure was really a great success.

A student of this science had set his mind on making a certain business combination, which seemed to him at the time to be very desirable, and he worked for some weeks to bring it about. When the crucial time came, the thing failed in a perfectly inexplicable way; it was as if some unseen influence had been working secretly against him. He was not disappointed; on the contrary, he thanked God that his desire had been overruled, and went steadily on with a grateful mind. In a few weeks an opportunity so much better came his way that he would not have made the first deal on any account; and he saw that a Mind which knew more than he knew had prevented him from losing the greater good by entangling himself with the lesser.

That is the way every seeming failure will work out for you, if you keep your faith, hold to your purpose, have gratitude, and do, every day all that can be done that day, doing each separate act in a successful manner.

When you make a failure, it is because you have not asked for enough; keep on, and something larger then you were seeking will certainly come to you. Remember this.

You will not fail because you lack the necessary talent to do what you wish to do. If you go on as we have directed, you will develop all the talent that is necessary to the doing of your work.

It is not within the scope of this book to deal with the science of cultivating talent; but it is as certain and simple as the process of getting rich in marriage.

However, do not hesitate or waver for fear that when you come to any certain place you will fail for lack of ability; keep right on, and when you come to that place, the ability will be furnished to you. The same source of ability, which enabled Barack Obama to be elected to the highest office in the United States of America, is open to you; you may draw upon all the Mind there is for wisdom to use in meeting the responsibilities, which are laid upon you. Go on in full faith.

Study this book. Make it your constant companion until you have mastered all the ideas contained in it. While you are getting firmly established in this faith, you will do well to give up most recreations and pleasure; and to stay away from places where ideas conflicting with these are advanced in lectures or sermons. Do not read pessimistic or conflicting literature, or get into arguments upon the matter. Do very little reading, outside of the writers mentioned in the preface. Spend most of your leisure time together contemplating your vision, and in cultivating gratitude, and in reading this book. It contains all you need to know of the science of getting rich in marriage; and you will find all the essentials summed up in the following chapter.

NOTES

IT IS THE CLOSE OBSERVATION OF LITTLE THINGS,
WHICH IS THE SECRET OF SUCCESS IN BUSINESS, IN ART,
IN SCIENCE, AND IN EVERY PURSUIT IN LIFE. HUMAN KNOWLEDGE
IS BUT AN ACCUMULATION OF SMALL FACTS, MADE BY
SUCCESSIVE GENERATIONS OF HUMANS.

– S. Smiles

Summary of the Science of Getting Rich in Marriage

There is a Thinking Stuff from which all things are made, and which, in its original state, permeates, penetrates, and fills the interspaces of the Universe. A thought in this substance produces the thing that is imaged by the thought.

Husband and wife can form things in their thought, and by impressing their thought upon Formless Substance can cause the thing they think about to be created.

In order to do this, husband and wife must pass from the competitive to the creative mind; otherwise, they cannot be in harmony with the Formless Intelligence, which is always creative and never competitive in spirit.

Husband and wife may come into full harmony with the Formless Substance by entertaining a lively and sincere gratitude for the blessings it bestows upon them. Gratitude unifies the mind of man and woman with the intelligence of Substance, so that their thoughts are received by the Formless. Husband and wife can remain upon the creative plane only by uniting themselves with the Formless Intelligence through a deep and continuous feeling of gratitude.

Husband and wife must form a clear and definite mental image of the things they wish to have, to do, or to become; and they must hold this mental image in their thoughts, while being deeply grateful to the Supreme that all their desires are granted to them. The couple who wishes to get rich must spend their leisure hours in contemplating their Vision, and in earnest Thanksgiving that the reality is being given to them. Too much stress cannot be laid on the importance of frequent contemplation of the mental image, coupled with unwavering faith and devout gratitude. This is the process by which the impression is given to the Formless, and the creative forces set in motion.

The creative energy works through the established channels of natural growth, and of the industrial and social order. All that is included in their mental image will surely be brought to the man and woman who follow the instructions given above, and whose faith does not waver. What they want will come to them through the ways of established trade and commerce.

In order to receive their own when it shall come to them, man and woman must be active; and this activity can only consist in more than filling their present place. They must keep in mind the purpose to get rich through the realization of their mental image. And they must do, every day, all that can be done that day, taking care to do each act in a successful manner. They must give to every man, woman and child a use value in excess of the cash value they receive, so that each transaction makes for more life; and they must so hold the Advancing Thought that the impression of increase will be communicated to all with whom they come in contact.

The men and women who practice the foregoing instructions will certainly get rich; and the riches they receive will be in exact proportion to the definiteness of their vision, the fixity of their purpose, the steadiness of their faith, and the depth of their gratitude.

The Beginning

EVERY DAY IN EVERY WAY, IÁM GETTING BETTER AND BETTER.
-- EMILE COUÉ

About the Authors

Sherman and Sacha have been married for over 13 years. Together they teach people on how to improve and repair their marriages, using their own real life story of love, gratitude, and forgiveness as a model. They have seven children and currently reside in the Seattle area.

A marriage is customized to the two souls that make up the union!

Come visit us at www.enjoymentcounselor.com or www.thescienceofgettingrichinmarriage.com

www.ingramcontent.com/pod-product-compliance
Lightning Source LLC
Chambersburg PA
CBHW072101280526
45788CB00006B/2351